Hot places

Contents

Teachers' notes	1
Hot weather	5
Postcard from a hot place – 1	6
Postcard from a hot place – 2	7
Hot places	8
By the sea	9
Food from hot places: pineapples	10
Food from hot places: sugar	11
Food labels	12
The rainforest	13
The hot desert	14
Weather in a hot place	15
Rainforest birds	16
Snakes from hot countries	17
Packing a suitcase – 1	18
Packing a suitcase – 2	19
Rainforest animals jigsaw	20
Desert animals jigsaw	21
Fish	22
Feed the eagles	23
Hurricane	24
Transport in hot places	25
The tourists arrive	26
Hot air balloon	27
Safari	28
Desert heat	29
Buried treasure – 1	30
Buried treasure – 2	31
Visit to India	32

Teachers' notes

The activities in this book aim to support the implementation of the National Curriculum for Geography, across Attainment Targets 1 to 5, at levels 1 to 3. The activities should not be seen as teaching tools in their own right, but as opportunities for children to practise newly-acquired skills and knowledge. To make the most of these activities it is important at the start that the purpose of each one is explained to the children. In this way they can focus on the key aspects of the activity rather than become sidetracked into 'colouring activities'. It would also be very useful to have a large globe and an atlas available throughout for use with the activities. Then children will become familiar with using both as a means of solving problems, for example 'Is Kenya a hot country?' The teacher can discuss where hot countries are to be found using the globe and the atlas.

Aims of this book

- To introduce children to key ideas and features of hot places.
- To extend the children's geographical vocabulary and knowledge.
- To practise simple mapping skills.
- To provide activities which highlight the links between the local area and hot places.
- To provide opportunities to practise basic skills in English and Maths.

Reproducing the activities

In most cases, photocopying on to white paper is quite adequate, but for some activities, such as the Postcard from a hot place (pages 6 and 7) and the jigsaws (pages 20 and 21) it may be worthwhile copying on to card or coloured paper. Similarly, the elements of these activities can be reusable, especially if laminated in clear sticky plastic.

Geographical background

The activities in this book may require an element of teacher input in relation to children's knowledge and ideas about hot places. Some of the key ideas which should be developed are:

- There are hot places in the UK as well as overseas.
- Hot places can be very wet or very dry.
- Hot places are found near the Equator, stretching between the Tropics of Cancer and Capricorn.
- Hot places have some features similar to the children's local area and some which are different.
- There are very important links between the local area and hot places. Food is one of the most important of these links but goods like cars and clothes are other examples.
- Hot places experience different weather conditions.
- The plants, animals, birds and wildlife of hot places are both similar to, and different from, local plants, animals and birds.
- Hot places sometimes experience extremes of weather, such as storms or hurricanes, which can be very dangerous and cause a lot of damage.
- People make journeys to hot places for various reasons, such as on holiday, on business or to visit relatives.

Notes on individual activities

Page 5: Hot weather

Aim: to encourage children to consider the wide range of weather conditions which are experienced in hot countries – hot and wet, hot and dry, and so on.

Preparation and practice: talk to the children about different types of hot weather. Encourage them to think about types of hot weather other than sunshine, such as thunderstorms, before they start the activity.

Extension: draw pictures of people in different types of cold weather – cold and wet, cold and dry, cold and windy.

Pages 6 and 7: Postcard from a hot place

Aim: to enable children to think about the wide range of leisure activities that go on in hot places.

Preparation and practice: encourage the children to imagine they are visiting the place in the picture. Discuss what can be seen, as well as what they might do while they are there. Make sure they realise that the school address should be written on the postcard.

Extension: children could design their own postcards to send to other class members.

Page 8: Hot places

Aim: to highlight similarities and differences between hot places and the local area.

Preparation and practice: discuss with the children what is shown in the picture and before they start the activity encourage them to say which features are similar to ones in the local environment and which are different.

Extension: look at pictures of hot places in books and magazines. What things do these places have in common with the local environment and what things are different?

Page 9: By the sea

Aim: to develop awareness of coastal environments in hot places, the features that may be present and the human activities that take place.

Preparation and practice: discuss the features shown in the picture. In what ways is it similar to seaside places in this country and in what ways is it different?

Extension: talk about what the different people in the picture are doing.

Pages 10 and 11: Food from hot places: Pineapples and Sugar

Aim: these activities are designed to highlight the interdependence of the UK with hot parts of the world. In this instance food is seen as the link.

Preparation and practice: the children will need a large sheet of paper on which to stick their pictures once they have been coloured and sorted. Encourage them to think about how the pineapples and sugar travel from other countries to the UK and then how they travel around within the UK itself. Make sure they understand that sugar starts as a crop called sugar cane, which is cut down, then sent to the factory where machines crush it to squeeze out the liquid sugar, which is then processed into the granular sugar found in shops.

Extension: look at the labels on other foods, especially fruit and vegetables. Where do they come from?

Page 12: Food labels

Aim: to demonstrate the large number of hot countries which supply people in the UK with their food.

Preparation and practice: children can bring in labels from a wide range of foods, though fruit and vegetables (tinned or fresh) are very good for this.

Extension: use a globe to point out where the countries named on the label are to be found. Children will need guidance on which are hot countries (mostly between the Tropic of Cancer and the Tropic of Capricorn) and which are not. The activity can be extended to 'Food from other countries'.

Pages 13 and 14: The rainforest/ The hot desert

Aim: to develop awareness that there is a range of different environments in hot places – the rainforest is hot and wet, the desert is hot and dry. As a result, the two places have different types of vegetation and are very different in appearance.

Preparation and practice: talk to the children about rainforests and deserts to help familiarise them them with terms such as oasis, river and so on.

Extension: look at other pictures of rainforests and deserts. Pick out similarities and differences with the drawings.

Page 15: Weather in a hot place

Aim: to encourage the use of symbols to represent different types of hot weather.

Preparation and practice: discuss the symbols and their meaning with the children. They will need guidance about hurricanes, in particular what they are and why their high winds are so dangerous. The children can design and make their own symbols.

Extension: compare a week of your own weather with the weather in the hot place.

Pages 16 and 17: Rainforest birds/Snakes from hot countries

Aim: to encourage the children to think about the wildlife to be found in rainforests.
Preparation and practice: ask the children to choose their own categories for sorting the birds and snakes, such as size, markings and so on.
Extension: draw pictures of other animals that live in the rainforest, such as monkeys, bats, lizards and frogs, and sort them.

Pages 18 and 19: Packing a suitcase – 1 and 2

Aim: to develop awareness of how hot weather will affect both the clothes children will wear and the games they can play.
Preparation and practice: the children need to think about the types of clothing they would need for a holiday in a hot place, as well as what other items, such as sunglasses, they might need.
Extension: pack a suitcase for a visit to a hot, wet place.

Pages 20 and 21: Rainforest animals jigsaw/Desert animals jigsaw

Aim: to encourage children to consider the wide range of different animals to be found in hot environments.
Preparation and practice: the pictures at the top of the page will help children match the jigsaw pieces. It may be helpful to look at coloured pictures or slides of some of the animals such as the camel, the capybara and ocelot before the children start the activity.
Extension: draw jigsaws of other rainforest or desert animals for your friends to sort.

Pages 22 and 23: Fish/Feed the eagles

Aim: to encourage children to think about food chains in hot environments, such as rainforests.
Preparation and practice: the children will need to colour in and cut out the fish before sorting them according to pattern. They can then be stuck on to the eagles on page 23. Are there other ways to sort the fish, such as by colour or size, in which case the labels on the eagles can be changed, for example, 'This eagle eats only yellow fish.'
Extension: draw different types of other animals to be sorted by your friends.

Page 24: Hurricane

Aim: to introduce children to some of the dramatic and dangerous features of weather in hot places.
Preparation and practice: talk to the children about hurricanes and how they affect the lives of people who live in hot places. Stress the dangers of very strong winds, as well as tidal waves and flooding as a result of torrential rain. Make sure the children understand what is in each picture before they colour and sort them.
Extension: draw other pictures to show what might happen when a hurricane or another type of tropical storm hits.

Page 25: Transport in hot places

Aim: to highlight the many different types of transport to be found in hot places.
Preparation and practice: let the children choose their own categories for sorting, such as in the air/on land/on water, or with wheels/without wheels or animal/machine. They may choose categories where a type of transport should be included in two of the categories, for example aeroplanes fly in the air but take off from the land. Venn diagrams can therefore be introduced as another way of recording the information, which allows for types of transport to be included in more than one category.
Extension: draw other types of transport which might be found in hot places, for example a train.

Pages 26 and 27: The tourists arrive/Hot air balloon

Aim: to highlight the range of activities and environments to be found in hot places.
Preparation and practice: the children are asked to imagine what different characters might be saying about a particular situation. Let them discuss what might be in each speech bubble, and make sure they understand that they only write the actual words spoken.
Extension: draw other scenes from hot places, such as a swimming pool or a mountain landscape and write speech bubbles for people there.

Pages 28 and 29: Safari/Desert heat

Aim: to encourage children to imagine what it would be like to live in a hot place.
Preparation and practice: before starting these activities discuss what is happening in each of the stories with the children. They can then propose different endings before choosing the one they prefer.
Extension: write stories about other adventures in hot places, such as a camel ride to an oasis in the desert.

Pages 30 and 31: Buried treasure – 1 and 2

Aim: to develop children's map-reading skills.
Preparation and practice: it is important that the children understand that the map shows an island in a hot place and that the footprints mark the route to the buried treasure. Discuss the different dangers shown in the boxes on page 30

and how these will affect the route. Where will they place the hazards?.

Extension: draw other possible dangers, such as swamps, lakes infested with piranha fish, thick forests, wide, fast-flowing rivers and so on.

Page 32: Visit to India

Aim: to encourage children to consider the order of events involved in a journey to a hot place.

Preparation and practice: discuss the pictures and sentences that will go in the missing spaces. In this context, they need to think about writing short, clear sentences. What details can be included in the picture and which need to be relayed by the text?

Extension: draw what might happen next on your visit to India. Children could use reference or picture books to research this.

National Curriculum: Geography

The activities in this book support the following requirements of the PoS for KS1 from the geography National Curriculum:

Geographical skills

Pupils should be taught to:
- extract information from, and add it to, pictorial maps;
- make representations of actual or imaginary places;
- follow a route on a map.

Places and themes

Pupils should be taught to:
- talk about work and leisure activities;
- investigate features of localities outside the local area;
- identify and describe similarities and differences between their local area and other localities.

Physical geography

Pupils should be taught:
- the effects of weather on themselves and their surroundings and to recognise seasonal weather patterns.
- about weather conditions in different parts of the world.

Human geography

Pupils should be taught to:
- investigate how people make journeys, why different means of transport are needed and why people make journeys of different lengths.

Scottish Curriculum Environmental Studies 5–14: Social Subjects

Attainment outcome	Strand	Target	Level
Understanding people and places	Knowledge and understanding	Aspects of the physical and built environment. Ways in which places have affected people and people have used and affected places. Transport and communications links and networks.	A
	Collecting evidence	By watching and asking questions, obtain information for a given task, eg observe weather variations from day to day.	A
	Recording and presenting	Record collected evidence by drawing pictures, making lists and pictorial charts, writing captions and short pieces.	A

● **Name** ______________________

Hot weather

● The pictures show two types of hot weather.
Colour them in.

Rain

Sunshine

● Now can you draw the pictures below?

Windy

Thunderstorm

● Name ____________________

Postcard from a hot place – 1

Use this sheet with 'Postcard from a hot place – 2'. You are on holiday in a hot place. This is the front of a postcard you are going to send to your friends at work.

● Colour it in.

Name ____________________

Postcard from a hot place – 2

Use this sheet with 'Postcard from a hot place – 1'.
This is the back of your postcard.

- Write to tell your friends what you have been doing.
- Now write your school address.

Name ______________________________

Hot places

- Look at the details in the picture.

- Colour in red the things that are the same as where you live.

- Colour in green the things that are different from where you live.

Name ______________________________

By the sea

- Colour in the picture.
- Can you match the words below to the objects in the picture? The first letter has been done for you.

hotel	sunbathers	beach
swimmer	boat	palm tree
sun	drink stall	cliff

Name ______________________________

Food from hot places: pineapples

These pictures show the journey of a pineapple from the field where it is grown to the shop in our country.

- How do we use a pineapple? Draw a picture in the empty space on the left to show this.

- Now cut out the pictures and put them in the correct order.

Name ______________________________

Food from hot places: sugar

These pictures show the journey of sugar from the field where it is grown to the shop in our country.

- Draw a picture in the empty space on the left to show a meal where you would use sugar.
- Now cut out the pictures and put them in the correct order.

Name ______________________

Food labels

- Colour in the labels.

- Can you find other labels from foods which come from other countries? Draw them in the space below.

Name ______________________

The rainforest

This is a picture of a rainforest.

- Colour in the picture.
- Can you match the words below with the objects in the picture? The first letter has been done for you.

tree	river	boat
cloud	rain	monkey

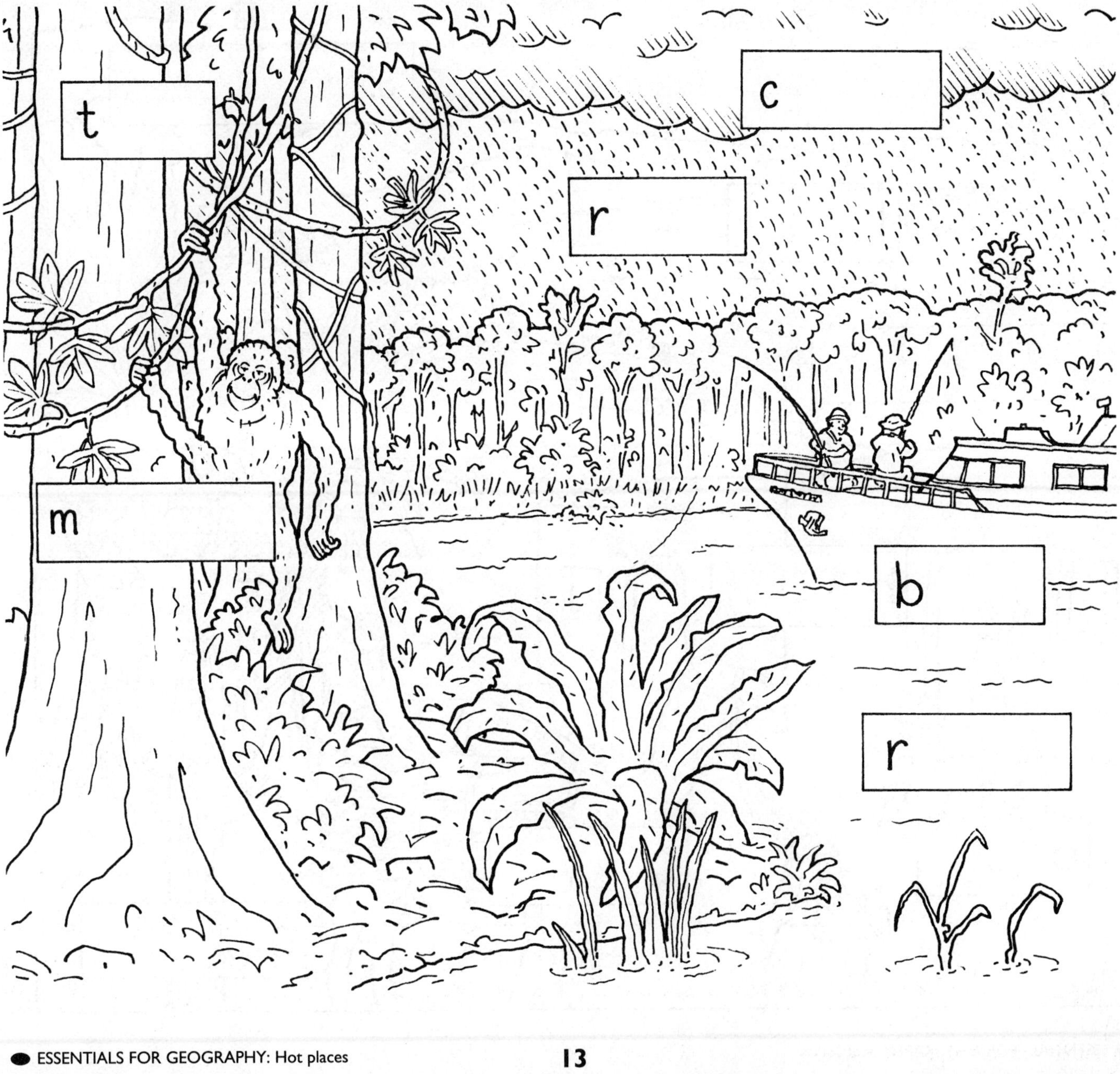

Name ____________________

The hot desert

This is a picture of a desert.

- Colour in the picture.

- Can you match the words below with the objects in the picture? The first letter has been done for you.

camel	**palm tree**	**lake**
cactus	**sand dune**	**dates**
house	**Land Rover**	**oven**
	oil well	

● Name ____________________

Weather in a hot place

This is a weather chart showing the weather for five days.

Day	Morning	Afternoon
Monday		
Tuesday		
Wednesday		
Thursday		
Friday		

Key

Sunny		Thunderstorm	
Cloudy		Windy	
Rain		Hurricane	

- What was the weather on Tuesday afternoon?

- What was the weather on Thursday morning?

- On Friday there was a thunderstorm all day.
Draw it on the weather chart.

● Name ____________________________

Rainforest birds

You can use this sheet with 'Snakes from hot countries'.

These are birds from the rainforest.

- Cut out the birds and sort them into groups.

●Name ______________________________

Snakes from hot countries

You can use this sheet with 'Rainforest birds'.

- Cut out the snakes and sort them into groups.

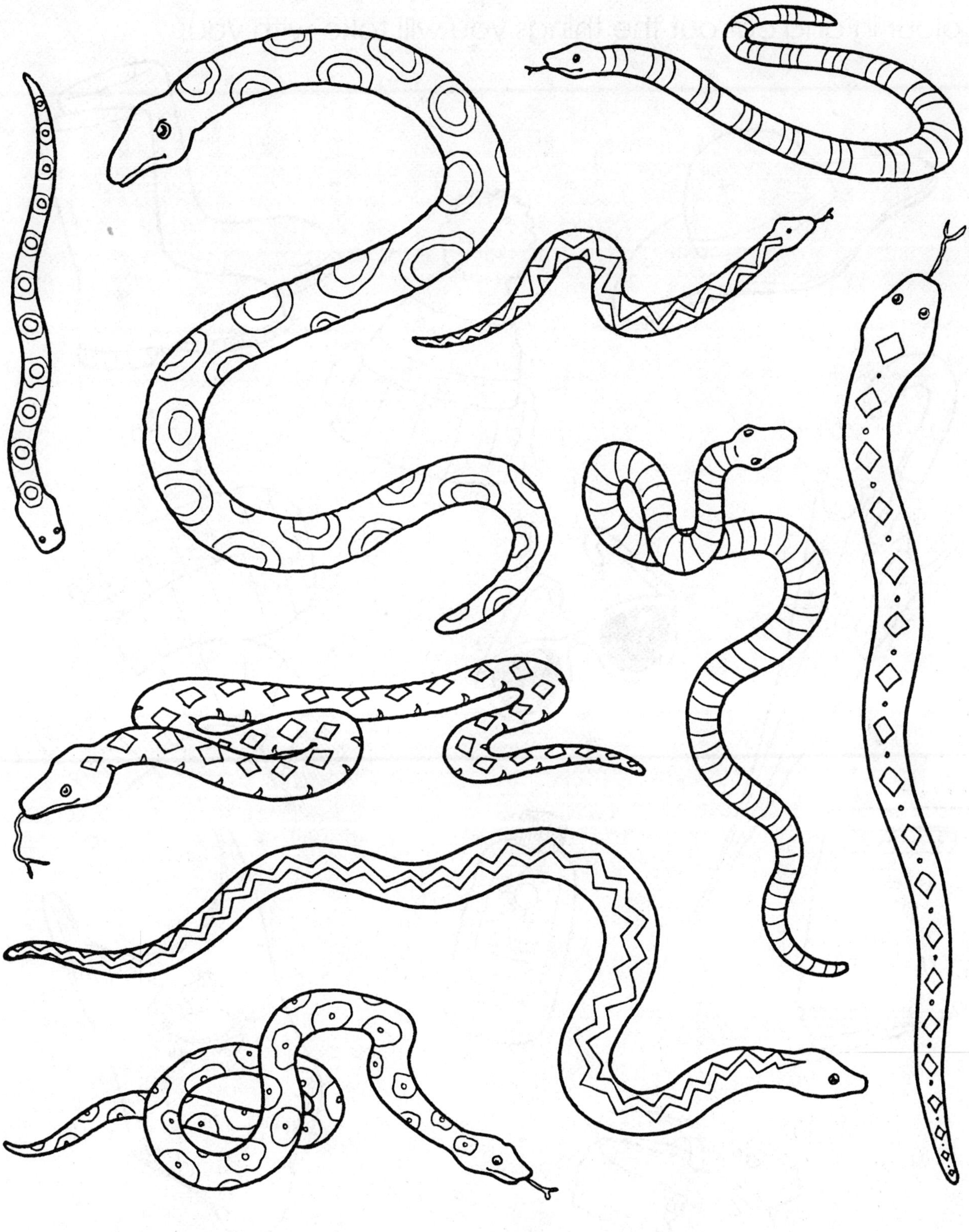

●Name ______________________

Packing a suitcase – 1

Use this sheet with 'Packing a suitcase – 2'.

- You are going on holiday abroad to a hot place.
- Colour in and cut out the things you will take with you.

Name ____________________

Packing a suitcase – 2

Use this sheet with 'Packing a suitcase – 1'.

- Stick the objects you will take on holiday in the suitcase.

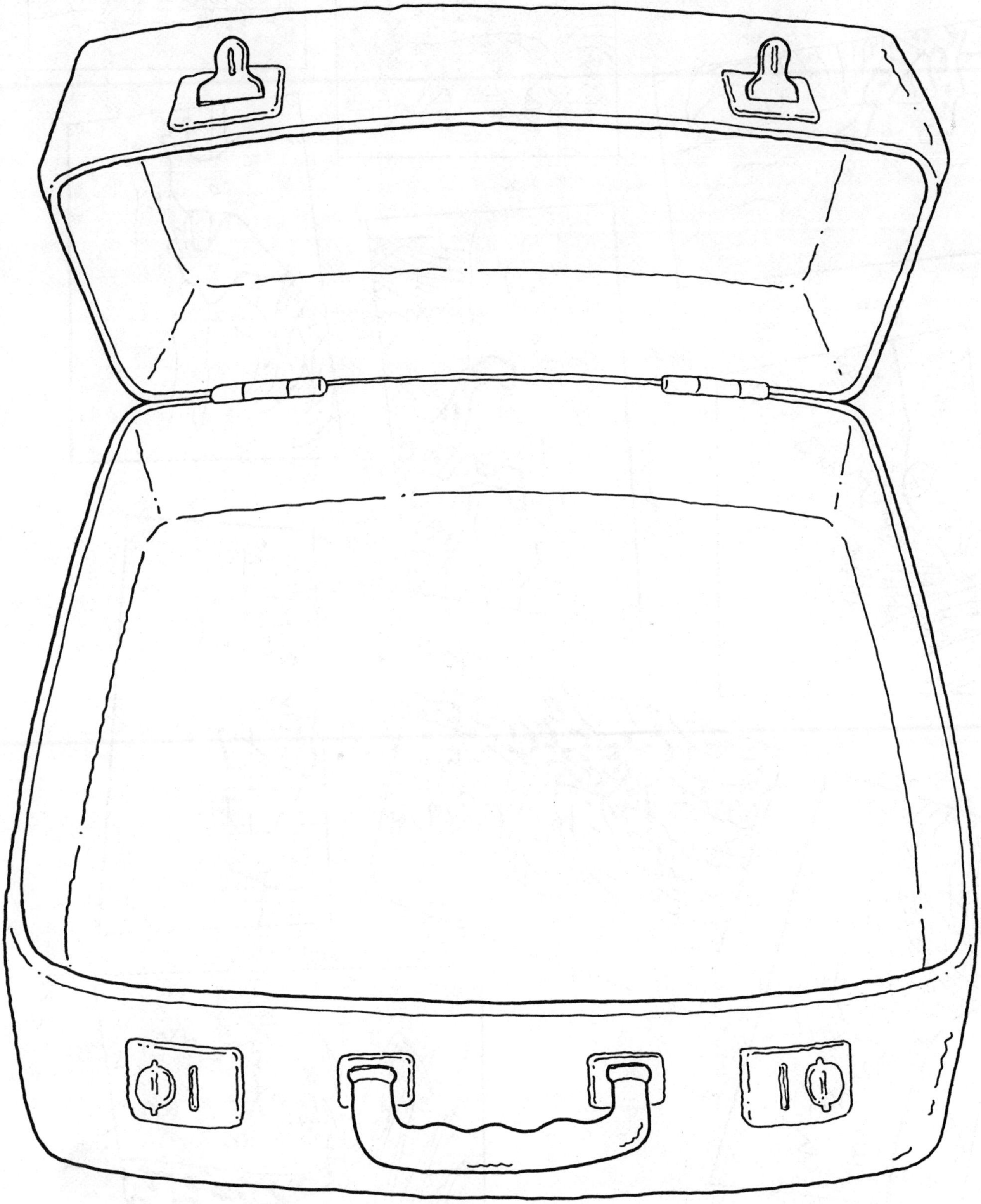

Name ______________________________

Rainforest animals jigsaw

- The pieces of two rainforest animal jigsaws have been muddled up. Cut out the pieces and complete the jigsaws.

● Name ______________________

Desert animals jigsaw

● The pieces of two desert animal jigsaws have been muddled up. Cut out the pieces and complete the jigsaws.

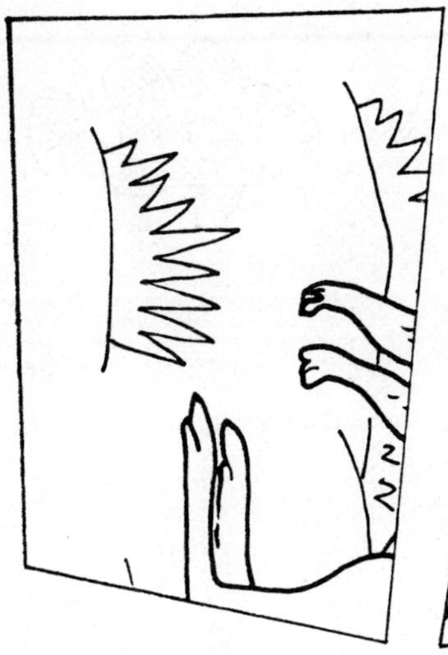

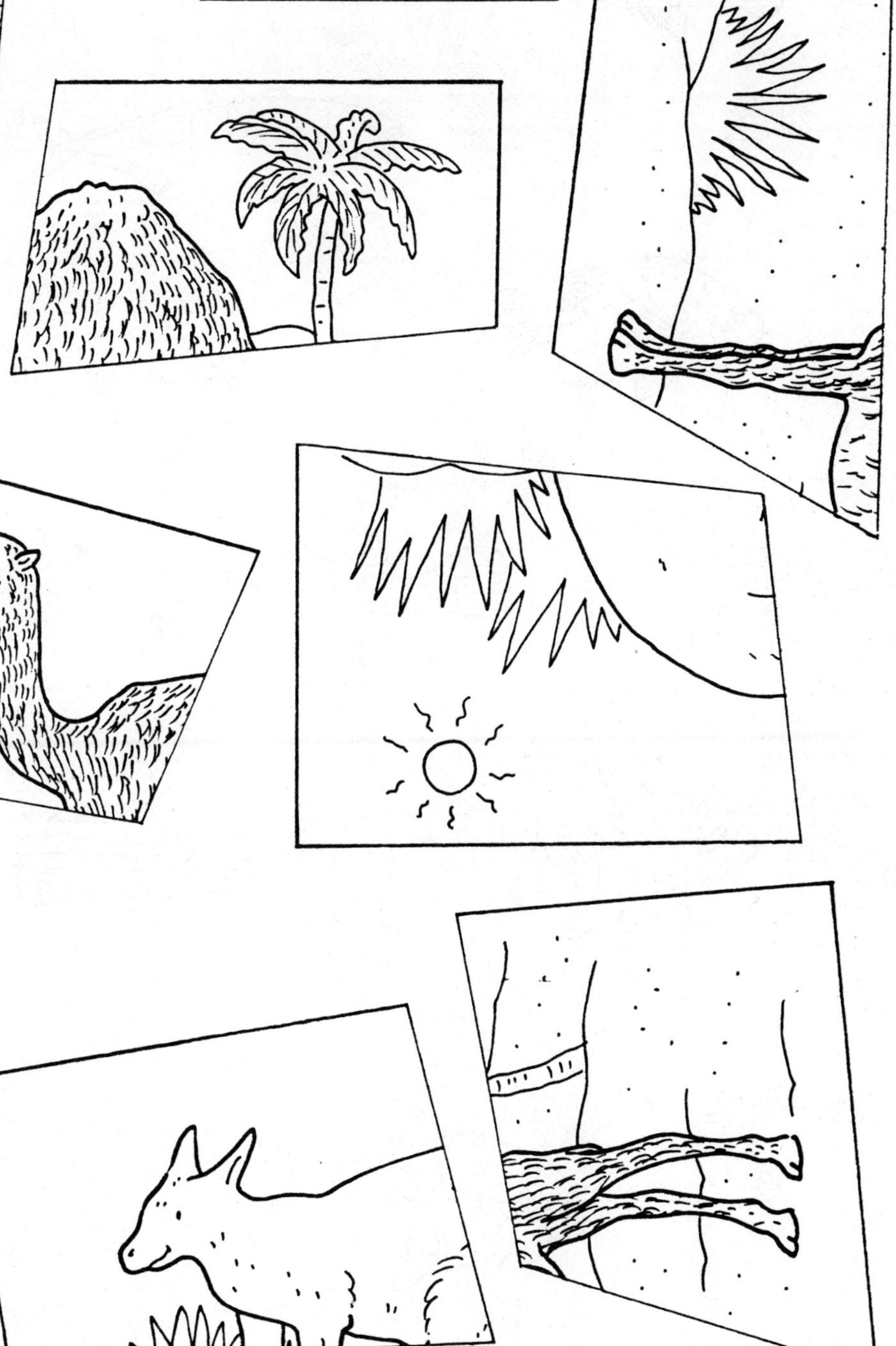

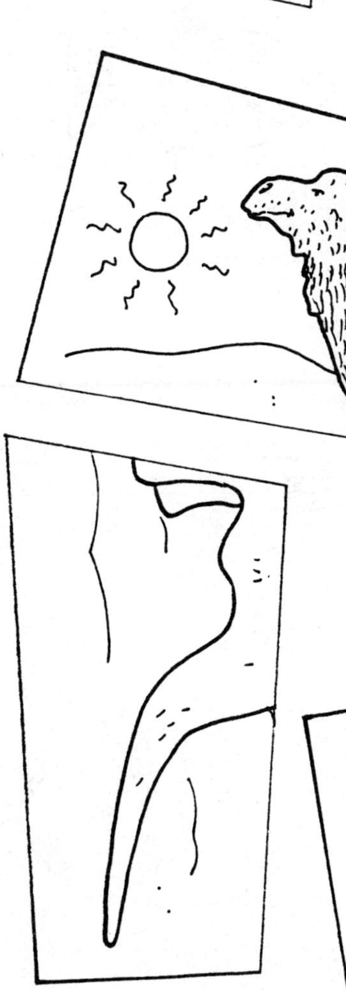

Name ______________________

Fish

Use this sheet with 'Feed the eagles'.

- Colour in the fish then cut them out and sort them into groups.

Name ________________________

Feed the eagles

Use this sheet with 'Fish'.

- Stick the fish inside the eagles.

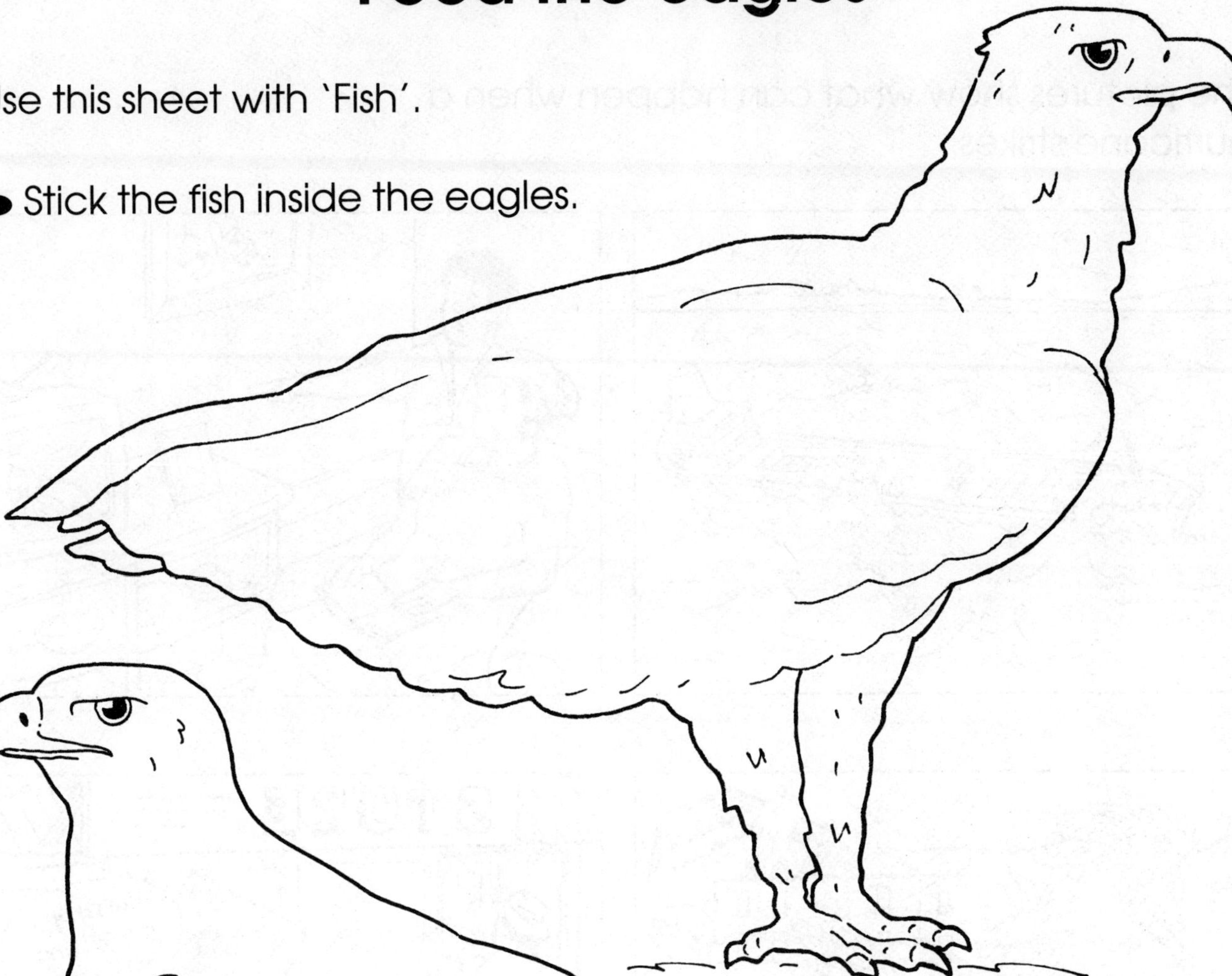

This eagle eats only fish without dots.

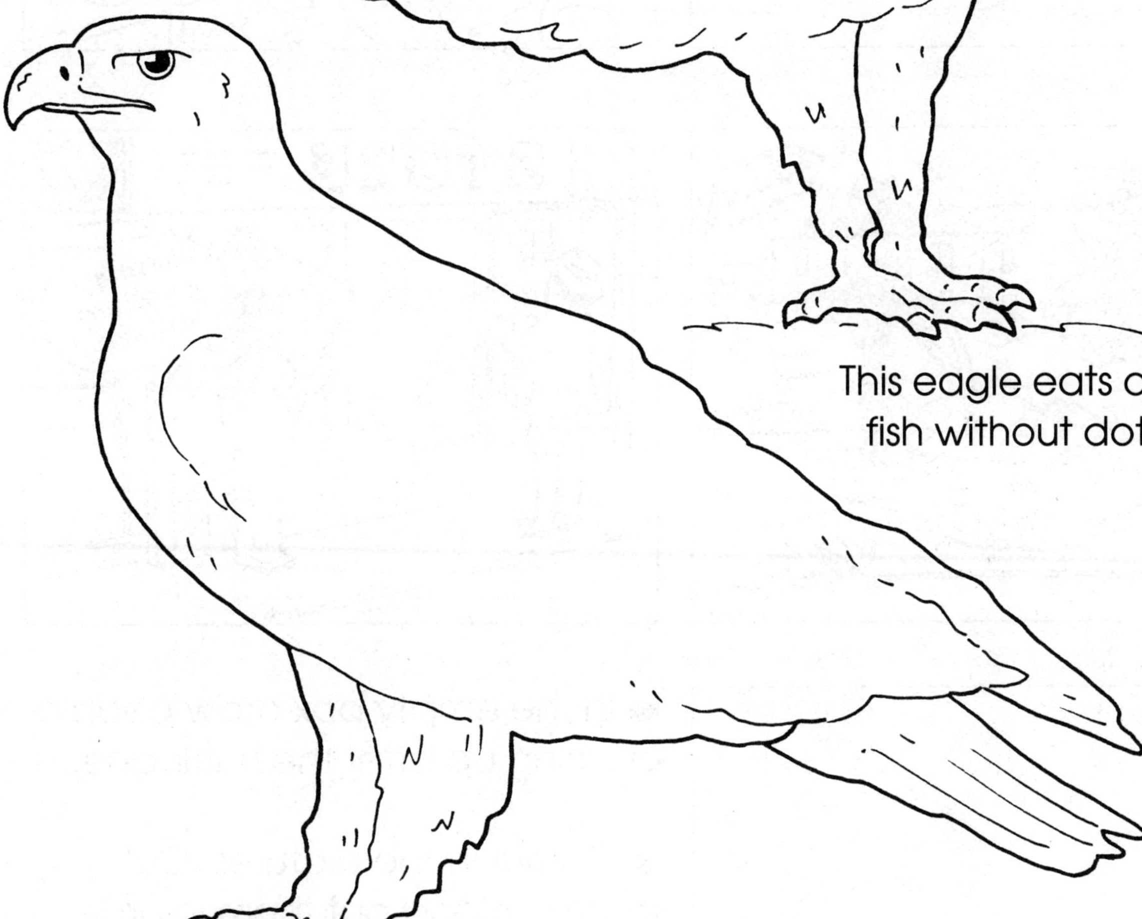

This eagle eats only fish with dots.

● Name ______________________

Hurricane

The pictures show what can happen when a hurricane strikes.

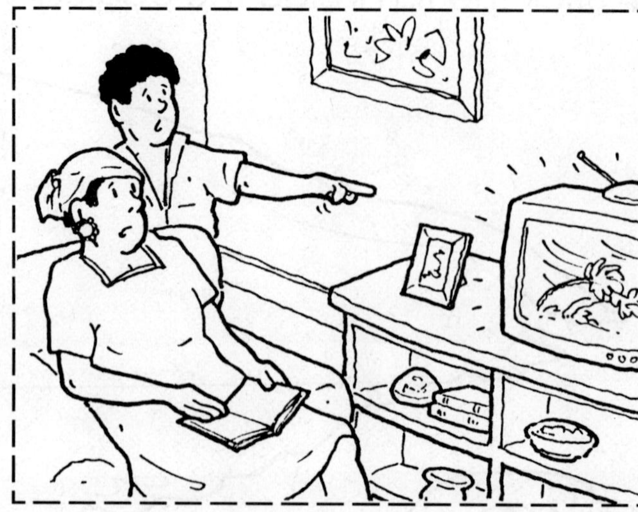

● In the empty box draw people clearing up after the hurricane.

● Colour in the pictures. Cut them out and put them in order.

Name ______________________________

Transport in hot places

- Cut out and sort into groups the different types of transport used in hot places.

● Name ______________________________

The tourists arrive

● Look at the picture. It shows tourists from a cruise ship on a day trip. They are visiting the island.

● What is everyone saying? Write their words in the speech bubbles.

Name ______________________________

Hot air balloon

- The people are flying over part of Africa. Look at all the wild animals.

- What are the people saying? Write their words in the speech bubbles.

Name ______________________

Safari

- Draw in the last picture to finish the story.
- Now give the story a title and write it out in words.

Name ______________________

Desert heat

- Draw in the last picture to finish the story.
- Now give the story a title and write it out in words.

Name ______________________________

Buried treasure – 1

Use this sheet with 'Buried treasure – 2'. It is a map of Dead Man's Island showing the route to the treasure.

- Look at the pictures below. They show the dangers along the route.
- Draw your own 'danger' in the last box.
- Colour in the pictures, then cut them out.
- Now stick them on the map.

poisoned water

no water

mountains

sand storm

____

Name ________________________

Buried treasure – 2

Use this sheet with 'Buried treasure – 1'.

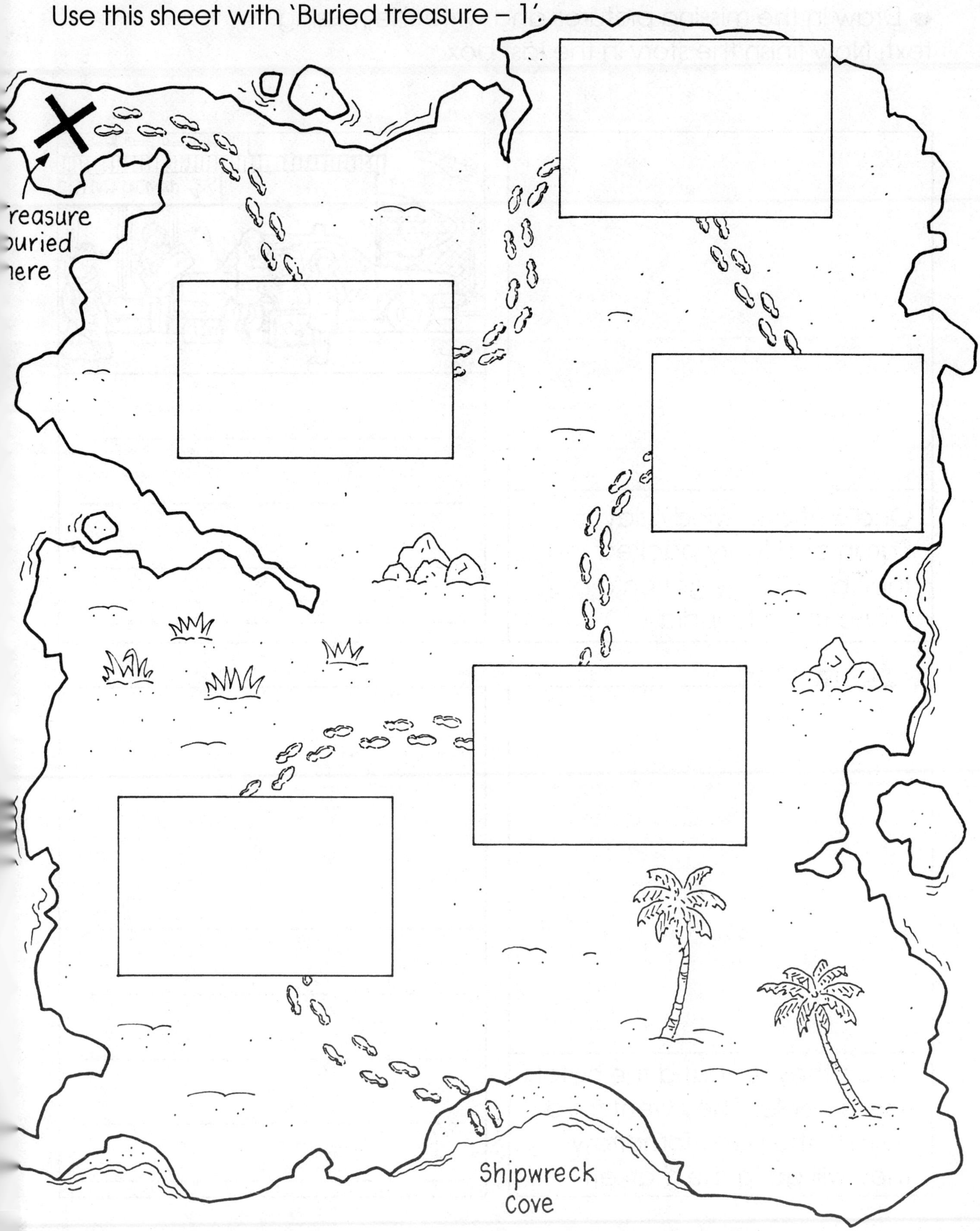

Name ______________________

Visit to India

Draw in the missing pictures and write the missing text. Now finish the story in the last box.

One wet and windy day Sarah and Mary packed their bags. They got on a big plane to go to India.

Once they reached the hotel it was cooler. They went for a swim in the pool. Tomorrow they will go to the market.

In the country

Contents

Country jigsaw	5	What am I?	19
Countryside game – 1	6	At the farm	20
Countryside game – 2	7	At the seaside	21
Country view	8	A village	22
Animal jigsaws	9	Farm animals	23
Machine jigsaws	10	Work in town and country – 1	24
Shepherd and sheep	11	Work in town and country – 2	25
Cow and calf	12	The river	26
Country journeys	13	Cliff rescue	27
Watching watersports	14	On land or water – 1	28
Wildlife park	15	On land or water – 2	29
Fire!	16	The farmer's day	30
Mountain rescue	17	The farmer's year	31
Wheat into bread	18	Seasons in the country	32

Teachers' notes

The activities in this book aim to support the implementation of the National Curriculum for geography, Attainment Targets 2, 3, 4 and 5, at Levels 1 to 3. The activities should not be seen as teaching tools in their own right but as opportunities for children to practise newly-acquired skills and knowledge. To maximise the benefit of these activities it is important that the purpose of each one is explained to the children at the start. In this way they can focus on the key aspects of the activity rather than become sidetracked into 'colouring activities'.

Aims of this book

- To introduce children to key ideas about the countryside.
- To develop children's vocabulary in relation to geographical features of the countryside.
- To provide study of a contrasting environment for children who live in towns.
- To provide opportunities to practise basic skills in English and mathematics.
- To encourage children to think about the links between their own lives and the countryside, especially in relation to food and leisure.

Reproducing the activities

In many cases photocopying on to white paper is quite adequate for the activities but in some instances, such as the jigsaws (pages 5, 9 and 10) and cards (pages 6 and 7), teachers are urged to consider copying on to card or coloured paper. The elements of these activities can then be reused, especially if laminated with clear sticky plastic.

Geographical background

To many children (especially those who live in towns and cities) the countryside is a great unknown. Their only experience of the countryside may consist of travelling through it on a bus, train or car. Similarly, many children still believe that milk automatically arrives in bottles or cartons and that bread comes sliced and wrapped. The link between food and farming is an important one which needs to be developed. Children often have little idea how the food they eat is produced. Activities which involve growing plants and seeds, such as cress, in the classroom are useful supports to a study of a rural environment.

Children need to know that farming takes place in the countryside and that it requires a lot of space. Other activities, such as leisure, increasingly take place in those rural areas which have particular characteristics, such as mountains, beaches or rivers. Food and recreation are the two most frequent topics through which children come into contact with the countryside.

Other significant features of study of the countryside include the importance of environmental dangers (pages 16, 17, 26 and 27) and the need to think about personal safety in such an environment. Similarly, the idea of changing seasons throughout the year and the effects of such changes on the environment may be familiar in relation to an urban environment but not within the context of the countryside (pages 31 and 32).

Notes on individual activities

Page 5: Country jigsaw

Aim: to acquaint children with the names and images of some of the key elements of the rural environment. Some children may be familiar with this already but to many it will represent new knowledge.
Preparation and practice: encourage the children to talk about the pieces of the jigsaw and to describe what each shows, using words like mountain, forest, field, river and village.
Extension: make other jigsaws of different country scenes for your friends to sort.

Pages 6 and 7: Countryside game

Aim: this game can be played with two or more children and helps to develop vocabulary appropriate for features of the countryside.
Preparation and practice: discuss why some labels are not appropriate to a scene, for example river and lake, to highlight differences of scale and shape.
Extension: make more cards with names and pictures of rural features, for example village, church, hedgerow, hill, pool.

Page 8: Country view

Aim: to extend children's vocabulary with particular reference to the human influence on the rural environment.
Preparation and practice: encourage the children to talk about features of the countryside and the animals found there. Which have been built or affected by man? Which animals are farm animals (raised by people) and which wild?
Extension: draw other country scenes and name the features, such as a farmyard scene with animals and farm equipment.

Pages 9 and 10: Animal jigsaws/ Machine jigsaws

Aim: to develop awareness of the types of animals and machines to be found in the countryside.
Preparation and practice: the pictures at the top of each page will help the children to match the jigsaw pieces.
Extension: draw and make other jigsaws of animals and machines for your friends to sort.

Pages 11 and 12: Shepherd and sheep/ Cow and calf

Aim: to encourage children to think about directions, a basic part of mapwork, in the context of two rural scenes.
Preparation and practice: there are different routes to be found through the mazes. Children can find the longest and the shortest routes and compare these with their friends.
Extension: draw different mazes of animals with their young, for example piglet and pig, foal and horse, for your friends to follow.

Page 13: Country journeys

Aim: to encourage children to think about different elements of the rural scene and the purpose or role of these elements.
Preparation and practice: this activity allows children to develop their skills of sentence writing, using ideas and objects appropriate to the countryside. Each sentence has a subject, verb and object.
Extension: write sentences about journeys in the countryside then cut them up for your friends to sort out.

Pages 14 and 15: Watching water sports/ Wildlife park

Aim: to encourage children to think about the countryside in relation to recreation. Most children first experience the countryside through leisure and these pages focus on some of these key leisure activities.
Preparation and practice: children are asked to imagine what different people are saying about particular activities and situations in the countryside. Discuss what the people might be saying. Ask them to suggest what might happen next or what the people in the pictures fear may happen next. Make sure the children know they have to put only the actual words spoken inside each bubble.
Extension: draw other scenes of leisure activities in the countryside and put in speech bubbles for your friends to complete, for example hill walking, mountain climbing and so on.

Pages 16 and 17: Fire! and Mountain rescue

Aim: to encourage children to think about some features of life in the countryside by focusing on two dramatic incidents.
Preparation and practice: many children see or hear about accidents in the countryside such as mountain rescue or farm fires from newspapers or television reports and these story-building activities are developed from this. Ask the children to write stories about dramatic incidents in the country using these pictures as a basis. Discuss what is going on in the first three pictures then consider what might happen next and how they might draw this. The whole story can then be written on the back of their sheets. Encourage them to use the appropriate vocabulary, such as river bank, mountain, tree, barn and so on.

Extension: write stories based on other dramatic incidents in the countryside, for example, cut off by the tide, a lamb stuck in a marsh.

Page 18: Wheat into bread

Aim: to make explicit the link between the food we eat and the farms from which it comes.
Preparation and practice: this is a straightforward sequencing activity using a topic which links food with the countryside. Discuss with the children what each picture shows. It may be necessary to talk about food and how food comes from farms in the countryside. Go on to explain how wheat is ground into flour to be baked into bread before the children start the activity.
Extension: draw a picture sequence of how peas get from field to freezer, or milk from cow to doorstep.

Page 19: What am I?

Aim: to develop children's knowledge and understanding of some key features of the countryside.
Preparation and practice: this activity is to encourage children to write short descriptive texts within a framework of the rural environment. Discuss the characteristics of the subjects before asking the children to complete the riddles.
Extension: write more of your own riddles based on elements of the countryside, such as plough, combine harvester, potato, strawberry.

Pages 20, 21 and 22: At the farm/At the seaside/A village

Aim: these activities are designed to help children realise that the countryside is a very varied place and that there are many different types of country scene.
Preparation and practice: these three activities are designed to (a) help children think about the range of different environments to be found in the country - from farms and villages to coastal scenes and (b) help children extend their geographical vocabulary in relation to these aspects of the countryside.
Extension: add other features to each scene which could be found in a farm, a village or at the seaside.

Page 23: Farm animals

Aim: to encourage children to think about the types of animals likely to be found on a farm. This is also a sorting activity.
Preparation and practice: children will need a large sheet of paper, divided into fields, on which to stick the animals. They could sort the animals in different ways according to size or maturity. Sorting activities could involve using a Carroll or Venn diagram.
Extension: draw and sort other types of non-farm animals to be found in the country, such as mice, foxes, badgers.

Pages 24 and 25: Work in town and country 1 and 2

Aim: to develop awareness of the types of work that people do in urban and rural areas.
Preparation and practice: encourage the children to talk about the types of work people do in the country and extend the discussion from jobs to do only with farming to occupations such as shopkeeping or painting. Children could sort the pictures and discuss the fact that some jobs are found in both town and country and so need to be included in the intersection where the sets overlap.
Extension: ask the children to draw people at work in other occupations, for example: fireman, nurse, gardener and so on, that they can sort into the correct section on the Venn diagram.

Pages 26 and 27: The river/Cliff rescue

Aim: to encourage children to think about the range of physical features to be found in the countryside, as well as to consider the dangers inherent in many of these features.
Preparation and practice: these activities encourage children to consider the sequence of activities involved in telling a dramatic story. In each case, a rural context enables them to develop their ideas of the main features of the environment, such as waterfalls and cliffs. At the same time ask the children to think carefully about how to summarise the action shown in each picture in a few short sentences. They can also consider which actions can be shown in the artwork and which can be described in the text.
Extension: choose a different rural location, such as a farm or mountainside, and develop your own stories.

Pages 28 and 29: On land or water 1 and 2

Aim: to help children identify the range of sporting activities which take place in different countryside environments.
Preparation and practice: discuss which sports take place on land and which in the water. Point out that some activities, like fishing, can take place on either land or water and so have to be included in the intersection on the Venn diagram where the sets overlap.
Extension: draw other activities which are land or water based to include on the diagram, such as bird watching or camping.

Page 30: The farmer's day

Aim: to encourage children to think about the work that takes place on a farm and how this

may vary during the day. The idea is to focus on the types of job involved.
Preparation and practice: ask the children to think about the different parts of the day, i.e. morning, afternoon, evening and night, then discuss what they do at each of these times. Sequence the pictures in linear or circular order and related to a clock face.
Extension: draw six boxes to show what you are doing at different times of the day.

Pages 31 and 32: The farmer's year/ Seasons in the country

Aim: to encourage children to think about how seasonal changes affect both the countryside itself (including the animal and plant life to be found there) and the jobs that take place in the countryside.
Preparation and practice: discuss the four seasons and the different activities which take place on farms at different times of the year. Ask the children to think of other farm activities, for example hay making in autumn, seed planting in spring. The children can draw their own pictures for each season to reassemble as a circle.
Extension: draw pictures of other countryside scenes in autumn, winter, spring and summer, for example a seaside scene, an arable farm, an orchard.

National Curriculum: Geography

These pages support the following requirements of the PoS for Key Stage 1 from the Geography National Curriculum:

Geographical skills
- observing surroundings and examining pictures and pictorial maps of distant places and using an increasing range of geographical terms, for example: hill, slope, river, road, house, shop;
- identifying similarities and differences between places, for example in the ways land and buildings are used and in the life and work of the people;
- extracting information from, and adding to, pictorial maps;
- following a route on a map;
- using pictures and photographs to identify features, for example homes, railways, rivers.

Places and themes
- investigating a locality in the UK which offers a contrast to the local area;
- talking about work and leisure activities;
- investigating features of localities outside the local area.

Physical geography
- identifying water in different forms;
- identifying familiar landscape features, including hills, rivers, ponds and woods;
- investigating the effects of weather on people and their surroundings and recognising seasonal weather patterns.

Human geography
- investigating the uses made of buildings in the local area and further afield;
- investigating how goods and services needed by the community are provided;
- understanding that adults do different types of work, for example teacher, bricklayer, bus driver, nurse;
- investigating how land is used in different ways, for example: farming, buildings, leisure.

Environmental geography
- investigating where common materials are obtained, for example wool from sheep;
- identifying activities which have changed the environment.

Scottish 5 – 14 Curriculum: Environmental studies: Social subjects

Attainment outcome	Strand	Target	Level
Understanding people and places	Knowledge and understanding	Aspects of the physical and built environment. Language and terminology of the area of study.	A
	Collecting evidence	Find simple pieces of information from pictures or written sources.	A
Understanding living things and the process of life	Knowledge and understanding	Variety and characteristic features: recognise and name common animals; interaction of living things with their environment: habitats.	A

Scottish 5 – 14 Curriculum: English language

Attainment outcome	Strand	Target	Level
Writing	Imaginative writing	Write a brief imaginative story.	A

●Name ______________________

Country jigsaw

This is a jigsaw of a country scene.

- Cut out the pieces and fit them together to make a picture.

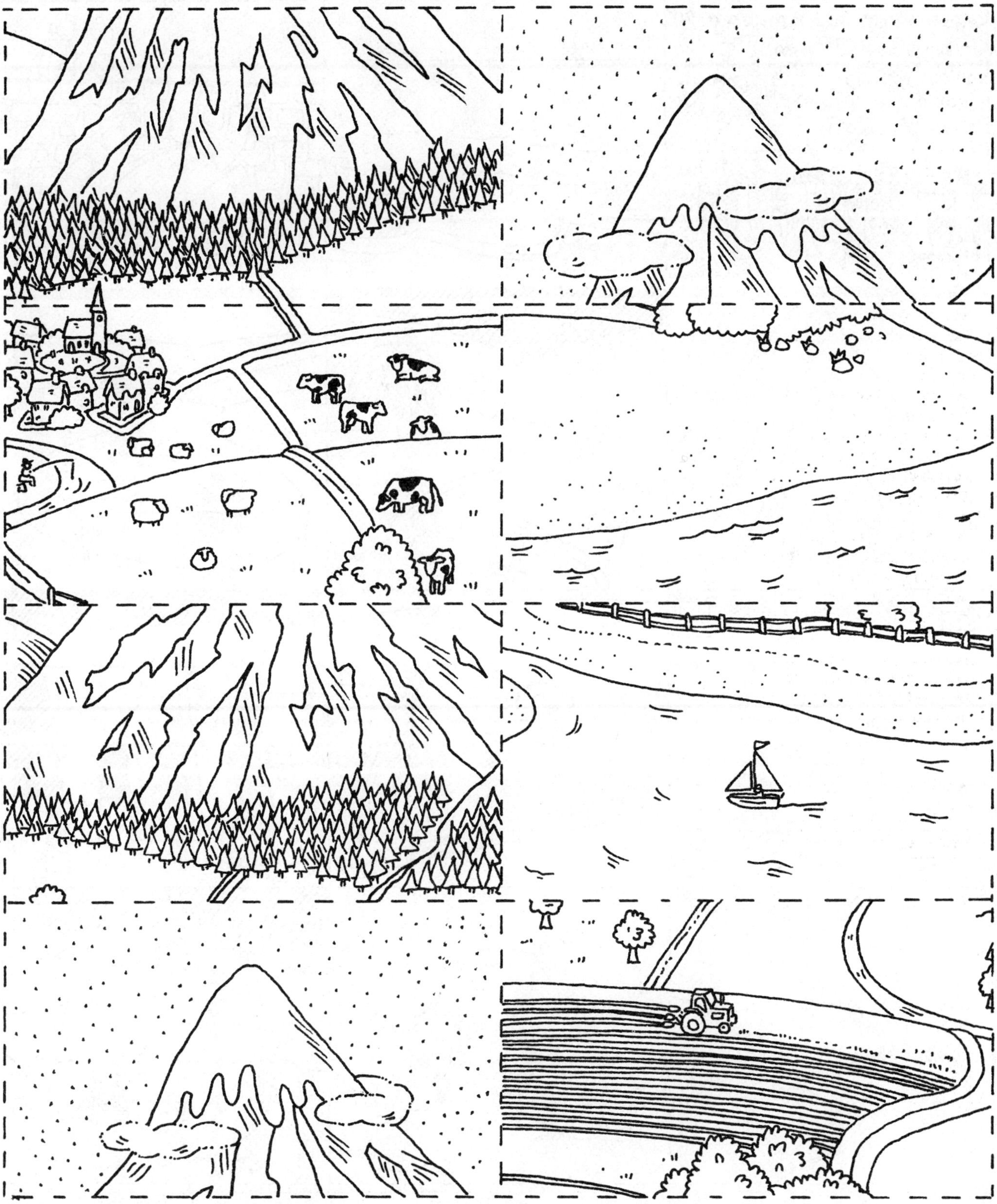

Name ______________________

Countryside game – 1

- Colour in the pictures and cut them out.

Use this sheet with Countryside game – 2.

Name ______________________

Countryside game – 2

- Cut out the labels and place them face down on a sheet of paper.
- Place the pictures from Countryside game – 1 face down on another sheet of paper.
- Take turns to turn over one card from each group. If the label and picture match you can keep them.

river	**field**	**quarry**
cliff	**beach**	**valley**
mountain	**lake**	**bridge**
sea	**wood**	**cave**

Name ______________________________

Country view

- Match the words with the pictures.

The first letter of each word is given to help you.
Write the words in the spaces provided.

field **cows** **sheep** **woods** **hill** **river**

bridge **hedge** **cloud** **sun** **bird** **fox**

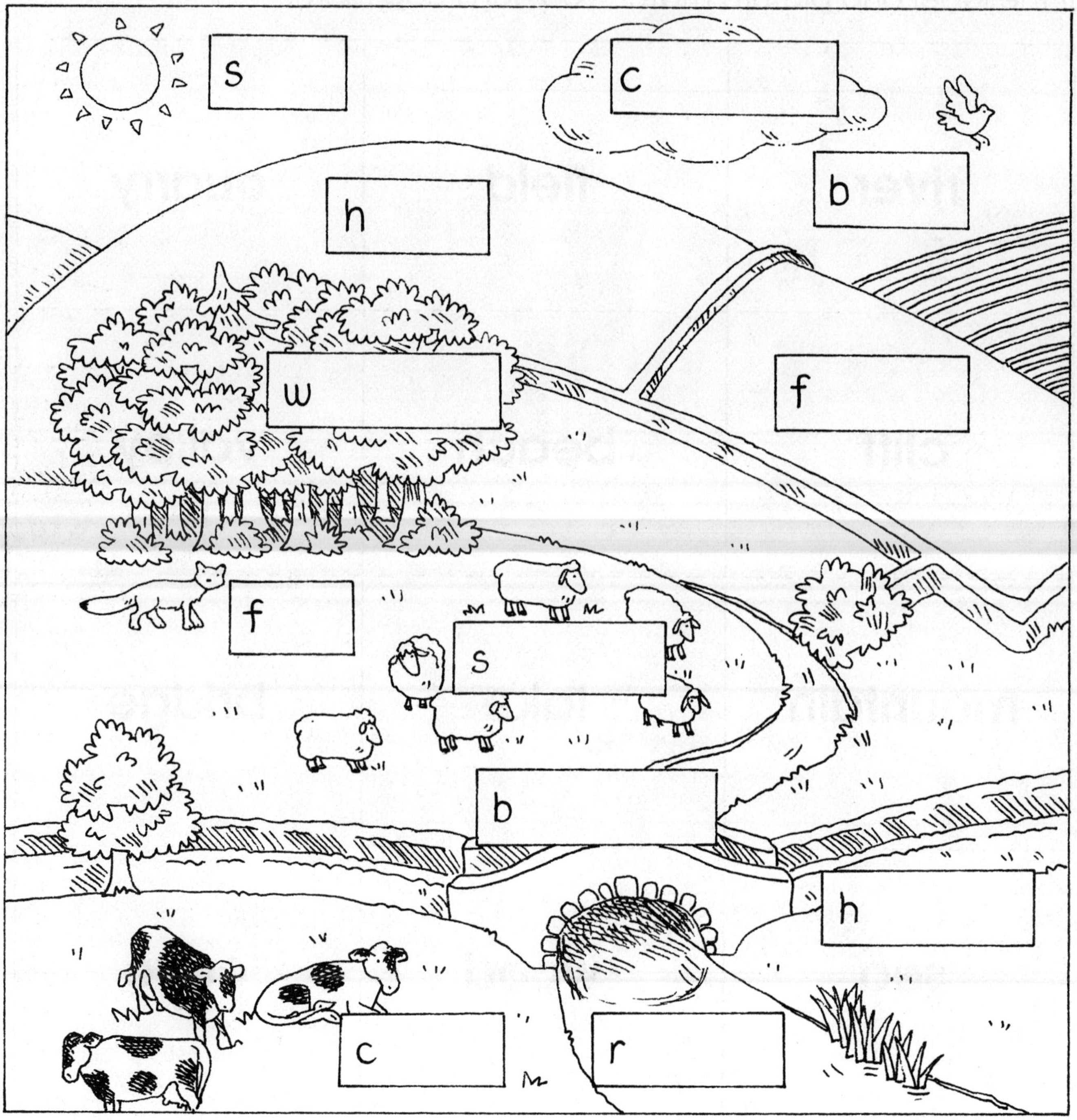

Name ______________________

Animal jigsaws

- Two animal jigsaws have been muddled together Cut out the pieces and complete the two jigsaws. The pictures may help you.

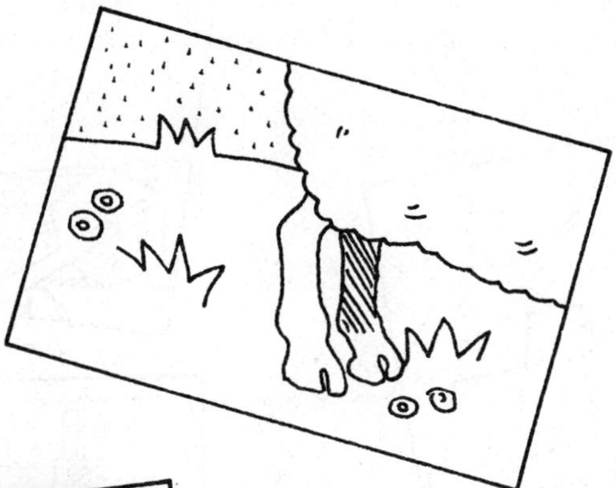

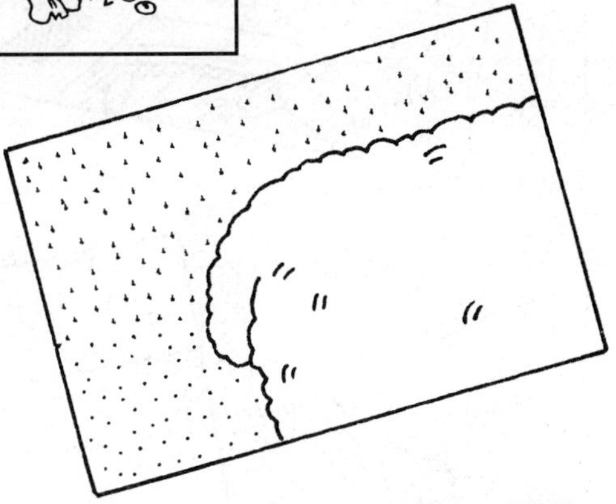

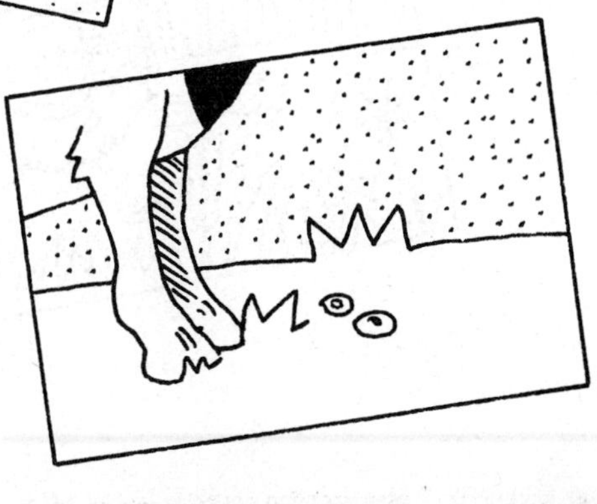

Name ______________________________

Machine jigsaws

- Two machine jigsaws have been muddled together. Cut out the pieces and complete the two jigsaws. The pictures may help you.

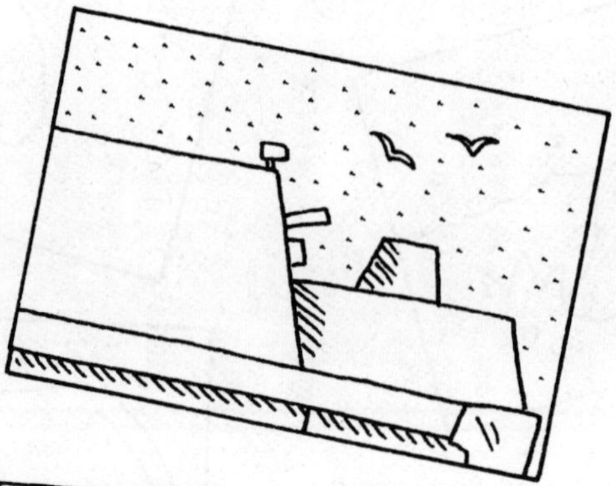

Name ______________________

Shepherd and sheep

- Find the route that takes the shepherd to his sheep.

Name ______________________

Cow and calf

- Find the route to take the calf to its mother.

Name ______________________

Country journeys

- Match together the two halves of each sentence then write the complete sentences on the lines below.

The cow walked	to the shops.
The farmer went	across the field.
The duck jumped	into the soil.
The plough dug	into the stream.
The bird flew	down the road.
The car drove	into the tree.

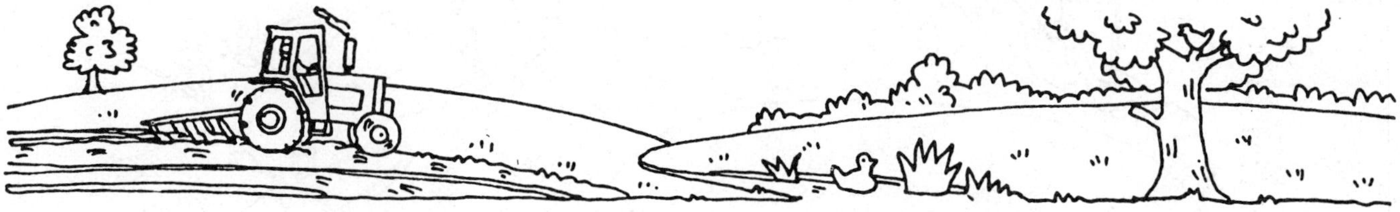

____

____

____

____

____

____

● Name ______________________

Watching water sports

● Look at the picture. What are the children saying?
Write their words in the speech bubbles.

●Name ________________________

Wildlife park

● Look at the picture. What are the people saying? Write their words in the speech bubbles.

Name ______________________________

Fire!

- Look at the pictures in the boxes below. Draw pictures in the empty boxes to finish off the story.

- Now write the story in words.

Name ______________________

Mountain rescue

- Look at the pictures in the boxes below. Draw pictures in the empty boxes to finish off the story.

- Now write the story in words.

Name ______________________________

Wheat into bread

The pictures show how bread is made from wheat.

- Colour in the pictures. Now cut them out and arrange them in order to show how bread is produced.

- In the empty box show how you might use bread.

Name ____________________

What am I?

- Can you solve the riddles and write in the answers?

I have four legs

People love my woolly coat

I eat grass

I am a ____________

I grow in fields

I am small, round and green

I grow in a pod

I am a ____________

- Now make up the beginnings to the riddles below.

____

____

____

I am a tractor

____

____

____

I am a cow

____

____

____

I am a chicken

____

____

____

I am a tree

- Make up your own riddles.

● Name ____________________

At the farm

● Match the words with the pictures.
The first letter of each word is given to help you.

pig	**tractor**	**farmhouse**	**barn**
cow	**farmer**	**combine harvester**	**field**

● Colour in the pictures then cut them out and make a farm picture with them.

Name ______________________

At the seaside

Match the words with the pictures.
The first letter of each word is given to help you.

harbour	lifeboat	pier	hotel
ice cream stall	fishing boat	fish	yacht

Colour in the pictures then cut them out and make a seaside picture with them.

Name ______________________________

A village

- Match the words with the pictures.

The first letter of each word is given to help you.

church	**school**	**cottage**	**garage**
bridge	**pond**	**horse**	**post office**

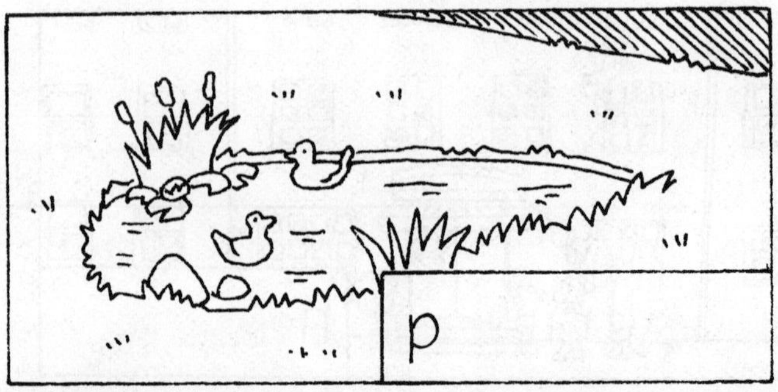

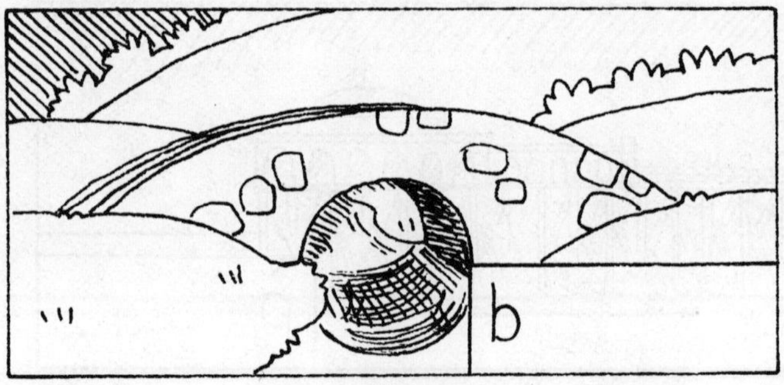

- Colour in the pictures then cut them out and make a village picture with them.

●Name ______________________

Farm animals

● Colour in the animals and cut them out.
Sort them so that each type of animal has its own field.

●Name ______________________________

Work in town and country – 1

Use this sheet with Work in town and country – 2.

● Look at the pictures below. Can you say what the people are doing? Which ones would you see in the town and which in the country?

● Colour in the pictures.

Name ______________________

Work in town and country – 2

Use this sheet with Work in town and country – 1.

- Look at the jobs shown on Work in town and country – 1. Write the names of the jobs in the correct section of the diagram below.

Name ______________________

The river

- Draw the missing pictures and write the missing text.
- Now finish off the story.

One windy day mum said 'You can go out to play but do not go near the river!'

____
____
____
____

At first, paddling the canoe down the river was easy. But when they turned to come back the current forced them towards the waterfall!

____
____
____
____

●Name ____________________

Cliff rescue

- Draw the missing pictures and write the missing text.
- Now finish off the story.

One sunny summer's day Rashni and Mike went bird-watching at the seaside.

Suddenly Rashni turned and saw the tide had come in. They were cut off!

Name ______________________

On land or water – 1

Use this sheet with On land or water – 2.

- Look at the pictures below. Can you say what the people are doing? Which activities take place on land and which on water?

●Name ____________________

On land or water – 2

Use this sheet with On land or water – 1.

● Look at the activities shown on On land or water – 1. Write the names of the activities in the correct section of the diagram below.

Name ______________________

The farmer's day

- Colour in the pictures and cut them out.
- Can you put them in the correct order?

In the late afternoon Mr Hadley drives the combine harvester.

After lunch Mr Hadley watches Joanne riding her horse.

First thing in the morning the cows are milked.

At night Mr Hadley sleeps.

In the morning Mr Hadley drives the tractor.

In the late morning Mr Hadley uses the computer.

Name ______________________

The farmer's year

- Colour in the pictures and then cut them out.

- Arrange them in order in the circle to show winter, spring, summer and autumn and write the name of the season in the space around the outside.

●Name ______________________________

Seasons in the country

● Read the sentences at the bottom of the page.
Can you match the sentences to the pictures?

In winter the lakes freeze over and birds cannot drink.

In summer people windsurf and row boats on the lake.

In spring lambs are born and trees get their leaves.

In autumn farmers plough the land and trees lose their leaves.

Routes and journeys

Contents

Teachers' notes	1	Going to Granny's	20
I come to school with	5	Going to the shop	21
On the way to school I saw...	6	Town and country – 1	22
On the way to school I heard...	7	Town and country – 2	23
Journey to school	8	Safety on journeys	24 - 25
Rush hour traffic	9	People and journeys	26
People who help on our journeys – 1	10	Letter to Switzerland	27
People who help on our journeys – 2	11	Routes from Ben's home	28
Crossing the road	12	Tracks and routes	29
Going on holiday	13	Journeys – 1	30
Crossing the road dominoes	14 - 17	Journeys – 2	31
Crossing the road safely	18	The crash	32
Accident!	19		

Teachers' notes

The activities in this book aim to support the implementation of the National Curriculum for Geography, Attainment Targets 1, 2, 3, 4 and 5, Levels 1 to 3. The activities are not designed to be teaching tools in their own right, but rather to offer children the opportunity to practise geographical skills and knowledge they have acquired. It is important to explain the purpose of each activity at the start, in order to focus the children's energy on that aspect of the task and to prevent the sheets being perceived as mere 'colouring activities'.

Aims of this book

- To highlight the many different journeys and routes children make on a regular basis.
- To help children think about the detail of those routes and journeys, in particular the main 'landmarks' along those routes.
- To demonstrate that the 'landmarks' people see on their journeys vary depending on whether they live in a town or in the country.
- To help children visualise journeys and routes as a sequence, with a start, a middle and an end.
- To encourage children to develop ideas about personal safety in relation to all journeys they make, but particularly in relation to their daily journeys to and from school.
- To encourage children to think about other types of journeys and routes, such as the journey of a letter.

Reproducing the activities

Most teachers will want to photocopy the activities on to white paper but with certain activities they may also consider copying on to coloured paper or card. This is particularly the case with pages 14 – 17 (Dominoes) and 24 - 25 (Snakes and ladders) where copying on to card and covering with clear self-adhesive plastic film will ensure that the materials have a much longer life.

Geographical background

Journeys and routes are a very important part of young children's geographical development. Journeys are the ways in which children explore their local environment (AT 2) and develop ideas about the buildings, people, rocks, roads and other features which make up that environment (ATs 3 and 4). Such journeys also allow children to develop basic geographical ideas about routes in relation to maps (AT 1) and to begin to think critically about the local environment (AT 5).

It is important to encourage children to think carefully about things they see on a regular basis in their local environment. Often, it seems that children walk or travel through the local environment with their eyes shut! It is vital to their geographical development for them to think about the landmarks, people and places in that environment, identifying the locations of those different places and people as well as considering their characteristics.

Taking children on short journeys around the school will encourage them to think about how to plan a route (for example, from their classroom to the hall), and to consider the things they will pass on the way. Providing guidance to a new member of the class (real or imaginary) on how to get to important places around the school, such as the hall or the secretary's office, can provide another stimulus for investigating routes and journeys. A short walk around the school grounds and into the immediate environment can be the next step in developing children's ideas about longer routes and journeys. In this way, a concentric approach can be adopted to the topic, in which children gradually investigate longer and more complex journeys as they grow and develop.

Other members of the family can also be involved in the learning process. The role of adults in helping children deal with ideas about personal safety is important, in addition to considerations about the different journeys made by different members of the family.

Notes on individual activities

Page 5: I come to school with ...

Aim: to encourage children to think about the people who form part of their environment. Immediate family members are the first to form part of this environment and the aim is to link this to the journeys children make.
Preparation and practice: the children are asked to draw themselves and a friend but they could go on to draw their own sheets for other friends. The person they come to school with should be an adult, so before starting the activity get the children to talk about which adults accompany them and why it is important to have help from adults over things such as crossing busy roads.
Extension: draw other adults seen on the way to school or on other journeys.

Pages 6 and 7: On the way to school I saw/ On the way to school I heard

Aim: to make children think carefully about things they see and hear on one particular route. This is also a sorting exercise.
Preparation and practice: the children will need a large sheet of blank paper on which to stick the pictures of the things they see, and hear, on the way to school. Use different coloured paper for things seen and for things heard. Point out that they should *not* cut out and stick in things they do not see or hear on their journey. Ask them to draw their own pictures of things they see, and hear, which are not shown on the sheets.
Extension: draw, colour and sort things you see or hear on other journeys, for example to the shops.

Page 8: Journey to school

Aim: to help children realise that journeys consist of a series of stages, and that one stage cannot start before the previous one has finished. Sequencing is a basic activity for understanding routes and journeys.
Preparation and practice: discuss what each picture shows before the children start colouring them in and selecting the correct sentences. They will need a large sheet of sugar paper on which to stick the sorted pictures. Can they draw and sequence pictures of their own journeys to school?
Extension: draw and sequence pictures of other journeys, such as to visit a relative or friend.

Page 9: Rush hour traffic

Aim: to encourage children to imagine what different people would say about a common feature of most journeys, in this case rush hour traffic jams.
Preparation and practice: discuss with the children what is going on in the picture and what people might be saying.
Extension: draw pictures of other common scenes connected with journeys, such as a visit to a bus or train station, waiting in an airport lounge and so on.

Pages 10 and 11: People who help on our journeys – 1 and 2

Aim: to focus children's thinking on people to whom they can turn for help on journeys and along routes. This is also a shape activity.
Preparation and practice: these are two cut, match and stick activities in which the figures at the top of the page should help the children arrange the different shapes in the correct order. Ask them to name the various shapes.
Extension: make other figures of people who help on journeys from similar shapes, for example a parent or bus driver.

Page 12: Crossing the road

Aim: to encourage children to think about personal safety in the environment. This is an important sequencing activity.
Preparation and practice: discuss with the children the correct way to cross a busy road. Ask them to talk about do's and don'ts. Discuss what is shown in each picture. Can the children arrange the completed pictures in a straight line sequence?
Extension: practise correct procedures for crossing busy roads in the hall or playground.

Page 13: Going on holiday

Aim: to encourage children to think about other journeys they make which are not as frequent as those to school or to the shops.
Preparation and practice: the sentences provide a simple outline for a story based on preparing for a holiday journey. Children can add their own sentences to continue the story on the back of the sheet.
Extension: write sentences for other, less frequent journeys, such as to the dentist or optician.

Pages 14, 15, 16 and 17: Crossing the road dominoes

Aim: to encourage road safety awareness.
Preparation and practice: copy the sheets on to stiff paper or card. Talk to the children about different ways of crossing roads. Make sure they understand the meaning of all the words involved. The game can then be played with groups of four children, each with one set of the dominoes. The winner is the first person to match up all their dominoes.
Extension: practise correct procedures for crossing busy roads in the hall or playground.

Page 18: Crossing the road safely

Aim: to encourage road safety awareness.
Preparation and practice: discuss what is shown in each picture and why it is a safe way of crossing a busy road. Use the pictures and labels for games of snap.
Extension: draw pictures and write the names of other features in the environment which help to cross busy roads safely, for example a crossing warden, railings beside a road directing children to a crossing.

Page 19: Accident!

Aim: to help children focus on what is safe and what is unsafe behaviour in the environment, linking the features of the environment to human activity.
Preparation and practice: ask the children to describe what is happening in each picture and look at why the accident has taken place. After they have sequenced the pictures the children can continue the story of the child's recovery in hospital and journey home with parents.
Extension: draw and sequence pictures of a different kind of accident, for instance what might happen to children playing a game of football near a busy road.

Pages 20 and 21: Going to Granny's/ Going to the shop

Aim: to encourage children to think about how routes change direction. Use right and left as ways of describing direction.
Preparation and practice: Going to Granny's – after drawing a route through the maze children can draw their own mazes. Going to the shop – revise left and right with the children before starting this activity. Make sure they understand on which parts of the picture they have to put the crosses and circles, i.e. where they change direction.
Extension: draw other mazes for routes, such as from school to the sweet shop or from home to the swimming baths.

Pages 22 and 23: Town and country – 1 and 2

Aim: to encourage children to think about how the same journey (i.e. from home to school) can be very different in different parts of the UK. The main contrast is between urban and rural scenes.
Preparation and practice: the illustrations from Town and country – 1 need to be matched with the correct section on the Venn diagram. You will need to explain that some objects can be found in both town and country and so need to go in the section where the sets overlap. Children can draw other objects to add to the diagram.
Extension: draw sets of things children hear on town or country journeys.

Pages 24 and 25: Safety on journeys

Aim: to focus on some of the dangers children face on journeys and how those dangers may be avoided.
Preparation and practice: the children will need coloured counters and a die to play the game. Copy the board on to an A3 sheet and make sure that children understand that they go up ladders and down snakes. Discuss how each picture shows either an element of safety or an element of danger.
Extension: add other pictures to the game to show elements of both danger and safety, such as running into the road after a ball or crossing safely with a crossing warden.

Page 26: People and journeys

Aim: to encourage children to look more carefully at people in uniform whom they see on their journeys. This will also link journeys with types of transport.
Preparation and practice: discuss with the children what vehicles and persons are shown in each picture before starting the activity. Talk about the job each person does and how it is related to journeys. Match the people with the vehicles.
Extension: talk about the job each person does and why it is important.

Page 27: Letter to Switzerland

Aim: to encourage children to think about different types of journeys, such as those made by parcels or letters.
Preparation and practice: talk to the children about sending letters to people in their own country and abroad. Discuss the contents of addresses and why these are so important. Make sure that the children know what each picture shows, and what homes in Switzerland look like.
Extension: draw and sequence pictures of other journeys, for example milk from farm to shop or doorstep.

Page 28: Routes from Ben's home

Aim: to begin the development of basic mapwork skills by focusing on key landmarks shown on a picture map.
Preparation and practice: make sure the children know where Ben lives and that the routes they draw must follow the roads. Talk about the things Ben will see on his journey, and the order in which he will see them.
Extension: draw a picture map of things passed on the way from school to home.

Page 29: Tracks and routes

Aim: to extend the idea of journeys from those made by people, to those made by animals.
Preparation and practice: talk to the children about the different tracks made by people, birds and animals and how these show up in snow or mud.
Extension: draw footprints of a bear or a dog to make a journey.

Pages 30 and 31: Journeys – 1 and 2

Aim: to encourage children to think carefully about the key landmark features in their environment and how these are important in journeys.
Preparation and practice: talk to the children about Journeys – 1 and show how the pictures relate to the words used in the boxes. Explain that the words in the boxes give an excellent summary of the journey, showing the places John passed and the order in which he passed them. Ask the children to use the four journeys on activity sheet 2 to summarise some of their own important journeys, for example from home to visit relatives or from home to school. Some children may prefer to draw pictures of landmarks they pass on their journey before they fill in the names of these landmarks on the sheet.
Extension: draw pictures of typical landmark features, such as shops, post office, garage, pub, road junction, park and so on.

Page 32: The crash

Aim: to encourage children to imagine journeys they or other people may make, taking into account what might happen and what the environment might be like.
Preparation and practice: this activity gives children the security of writing a story based on pictures. Discuss with them what each picture shows and how the story of the journey might end. In particular talk about what pictures might be in each box and how this will affect what they write.
Extension: draw a picture story of other journeys for friends to complete.

National Curriculum: Geography

The activities in this book support the following requirements of the PoS for KS1 from the geography National Curriculum:

Geographical skills
- following directions, including the terms forwards and backwards, up and down, left and right;
- extracting information from, and adding it to, pictorial maps;
- following a route on a map;
- making a map of a short route, showing main features in the correct order.

Places and themes
- identifying and naming familiar features in the local area;
- investigating the use of land and buildings in the local area.

Human geography
- investigating the uses made of buildings in the local area or further afield;
- investigating how people make journeys, why different means of transport are needed and why people make journeys of different lengths.

Environmental geography
- identifying activities which have changed the environment and considering ways in which the environment can be improved.

Scottish Curriculum Environmental Studies 5–14: Social Subjects

Attainment outcome	Strand	Target	Level
Understanding people and places	Knowledge and understanding	Aspects of the physical and built environment; locations, linkages and networks; using maps.	A
	Interpreting and evaluation	From recorded information answer simple questions about context and meaning.	A
Healthy and safe living	Knowledge and understanding	Safety in the environment.	A
	Taking action on health and safety	Investigate which people are important to health and safety	A

Name ______________________

I come to school with...

- Draw a picture of yourself in the first box.

- Now draw a picture of a grown-up you come to school with in the box below.

- Draw a friend in the second box.

- Draw a picture of a grown-up they come to school with.

Name ______________________________

On the way to school I saw...

- Colour in and cut out the things you see on your way to school.

- Stick them on to a large piece of paper.

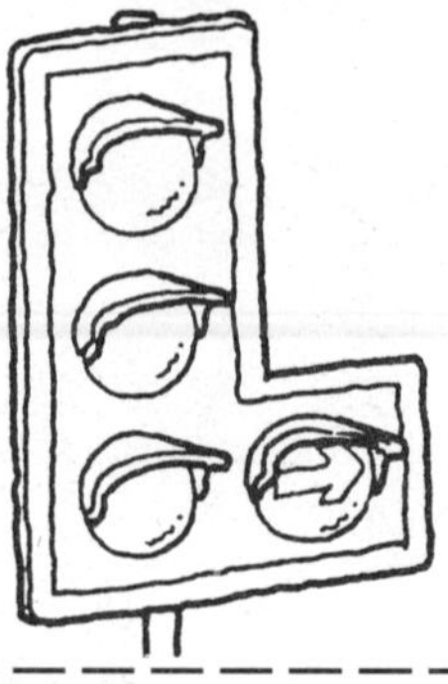

Name ______________________

On the way to school I heard...

- Colour in and cut out all the things you heard on your way to school.
- Stick them on to a large piece of paper.

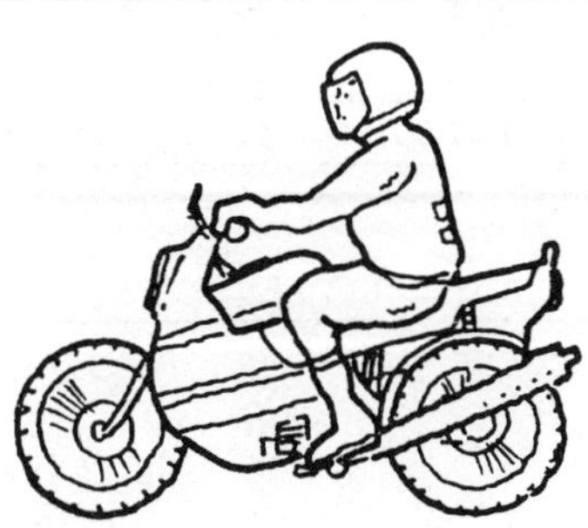

Name ______________________

Journey to school

The pictures show a journey to school.

- Choose the correct sentence from the list below to write under each picture.

Getting off the bus	**Waiting for the bus**
Getting on the bus	**Crossing the road to school**

- Colour in the pictures then cut them out and put them in order.

● Name ______________________

Rush hour traffic

The picture shows the rush hour in town.

● Look at the picture. What is everyone saying?
Write their words in the speech bubbles.

● Name ____________________

People who help on our journeys – 1

● Colour in the shapes below and then cut them out.

● Now can you stick them together to make a person who helps us cross the road?

Name ______________________

People who help on our journeys – 2

- Colour in the shapes below and then cut them out.

- Now can you stick them together to make a policeman?

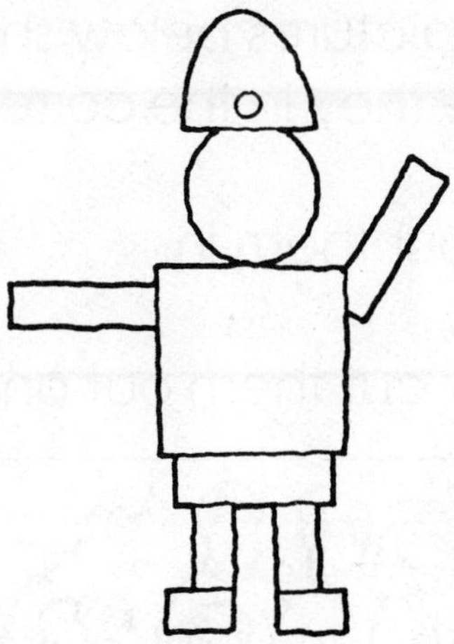

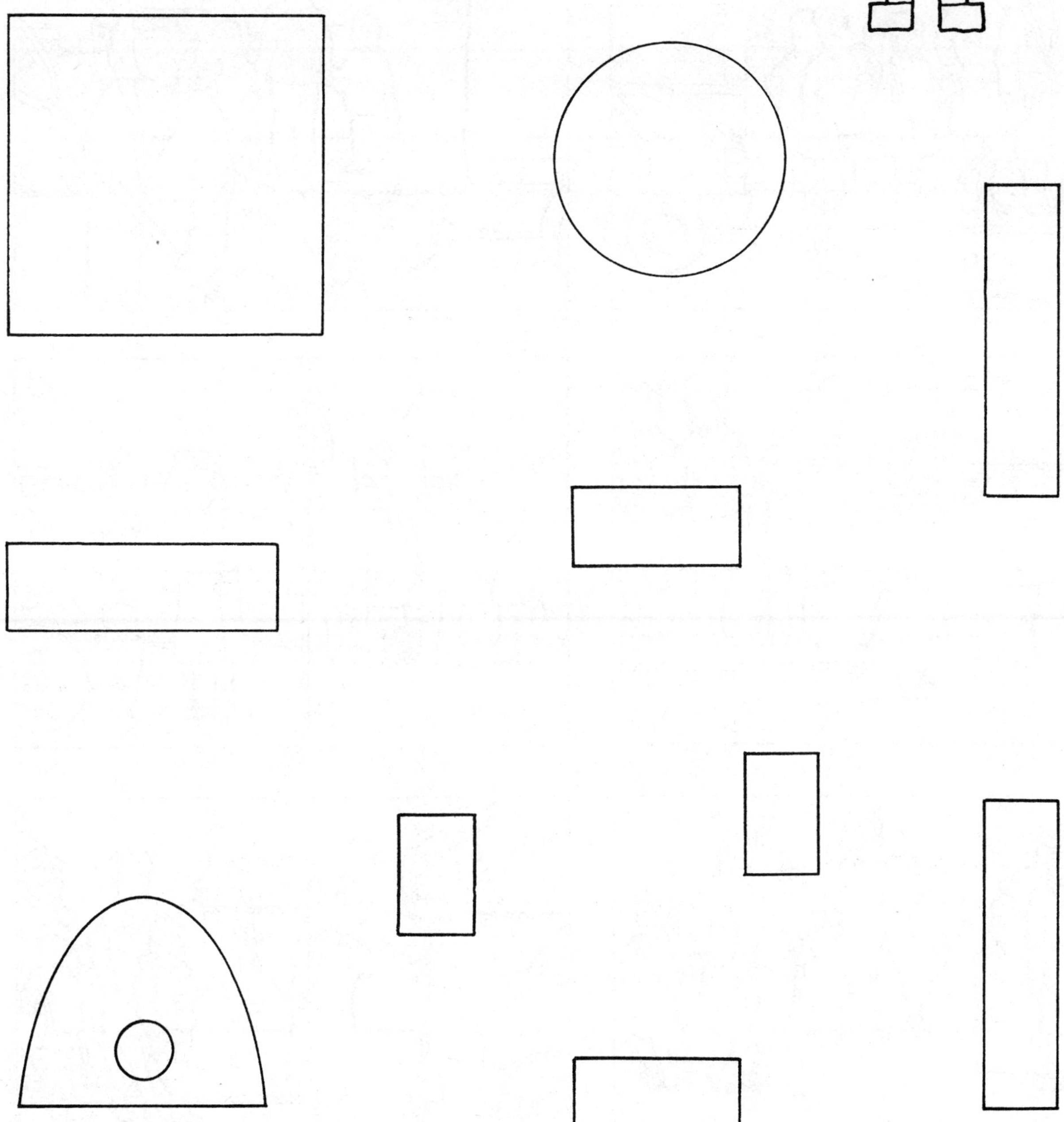

● Name ______________________

Crossing the road

● The pictures below show how to cross the road but are they in the correct order?

● Colour them in.

● Now cut them out and arrange them in the correct order.

Name ________________________

Going on holiday

Look at the sentences below and sentence endings beside the picture. Can you match them together to make a story? Write the endings in the correct spaces.

On the day we went on holiday ________________________

I dressed ________________________

I could not find ________________________

I looked ________________________

I thought ________________________

Then dad said ________________________

Sure enough, ________________________

in a hurry.

I woke up early.

'Look under the bed.'

my camera.

'I have lost it.'

in the cupboard.

there was my camera.

Name ______________________

Crossing the road dominoes – 1

- Cut out the cards on pages 14, 15, 16 and 17 to use as dominoes.

foot bridge

pedestrian island

traffic lights

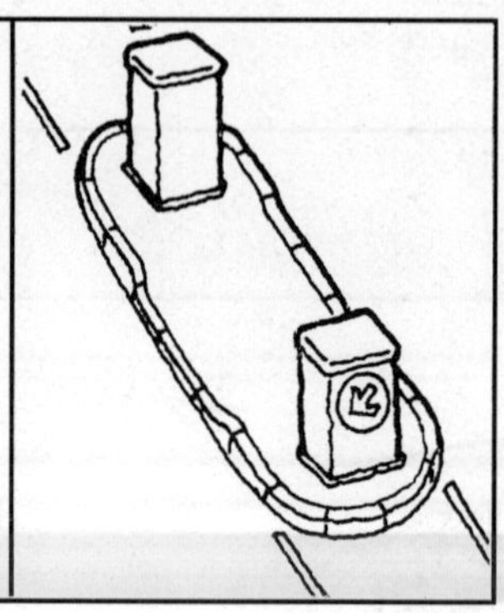

subway

pelican crossing

zebra crossing

Name ______________________

Crossing the road dominoes – 2

foot
bridge

zebra
crossing

subway

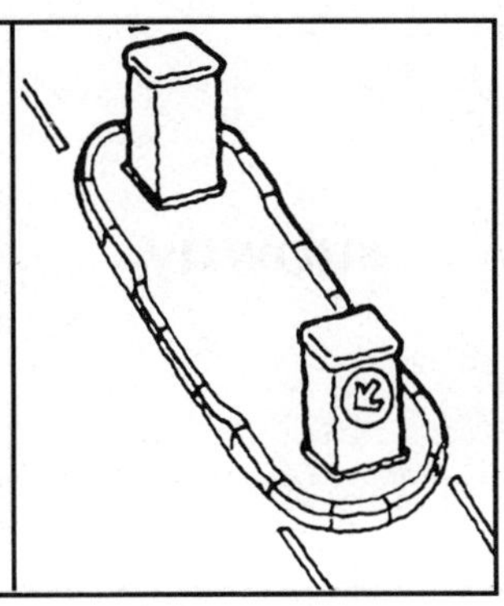

pedestrian
island

pelican
crossing

traffic
lights

● Name ______________________

Crossing the road dominoes – 3

traffic lights

pedestrian island

pelican crossing

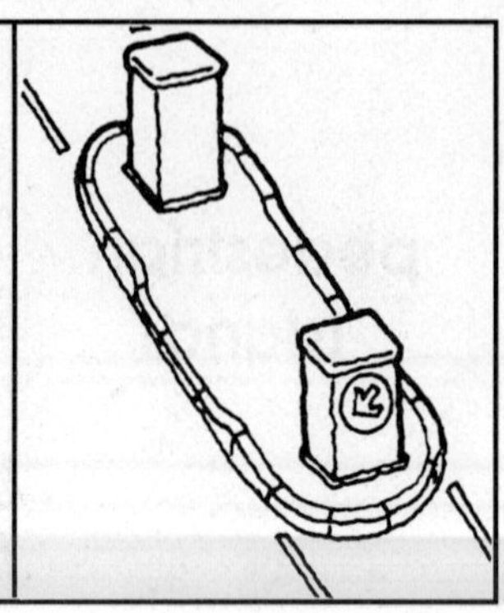

subway

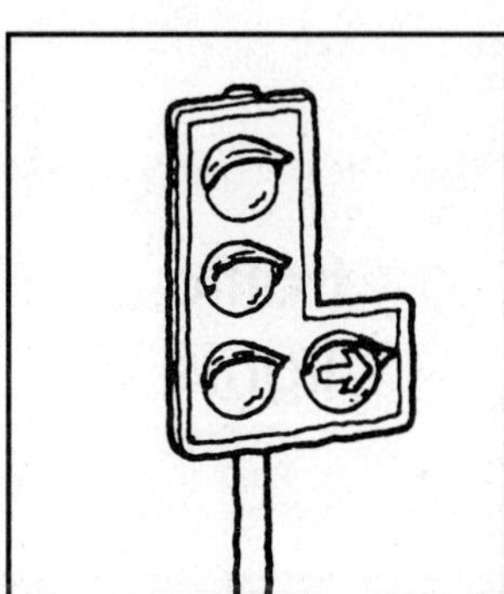

zebra crossing

foot bridge

Name ______________________

Crossing the road dominoes – 4

subway

pelican crossing

traffic lights

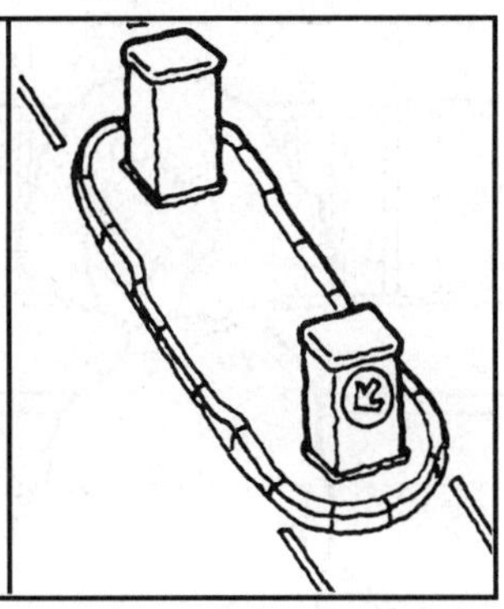

zebra crossing

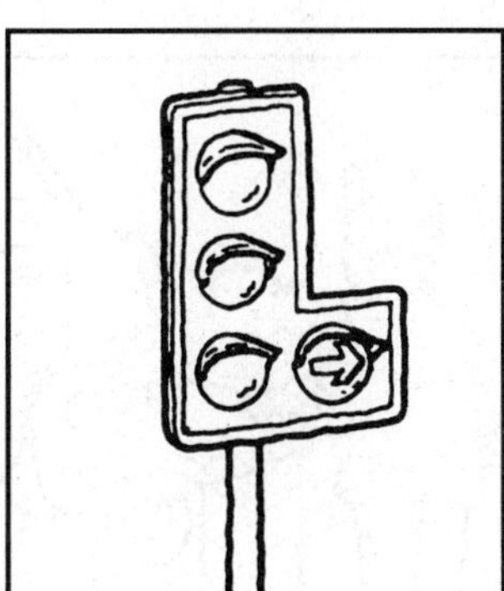

pedestrian island

foot bridge

Name ______________________

Crossing the road safely

The pictures show different ways of crossing the road.

Can you match the pictures with the labels?

pelican crossing

foot bridge

pedestrian island

zebra crossing

subway

Name ____________________

Accident!

The pictures show the story of a child who has an accident.

- Colour in the pictures.

- Now cut them out and put them in order to make a story.

● Name ______________________

Going to Granny's

● Help Linda find her way to Granny's house.
Which route will she need to take?

● Name ______________________________

Going to the shop

- Follow the path from Sophie's home to the shop.
- Put 'O' at every right turn.
- Put 'X' at every left turn.

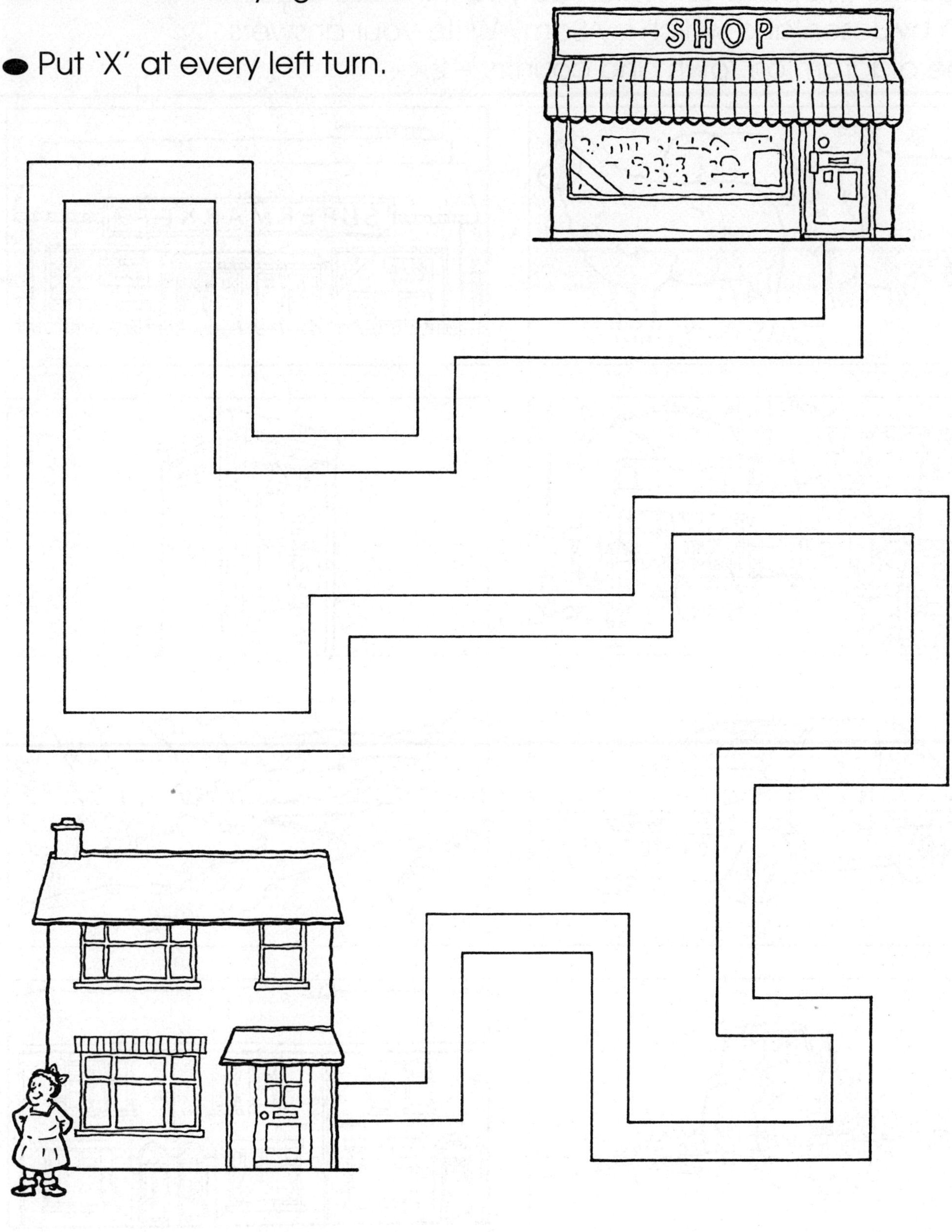

● Name ______________________

Town and country – 1

Jason lives in a town. Sam lives in the country.

● Look at the pictures. Which do you think are usually seen by Jason and which by Sam? Write your answers in the diagram on Town and country – 2.

Name ______________________

Town and country – 2

- Use this sheet with Town and country – 1.

● Name ______________________________

Safety on journeys – 1

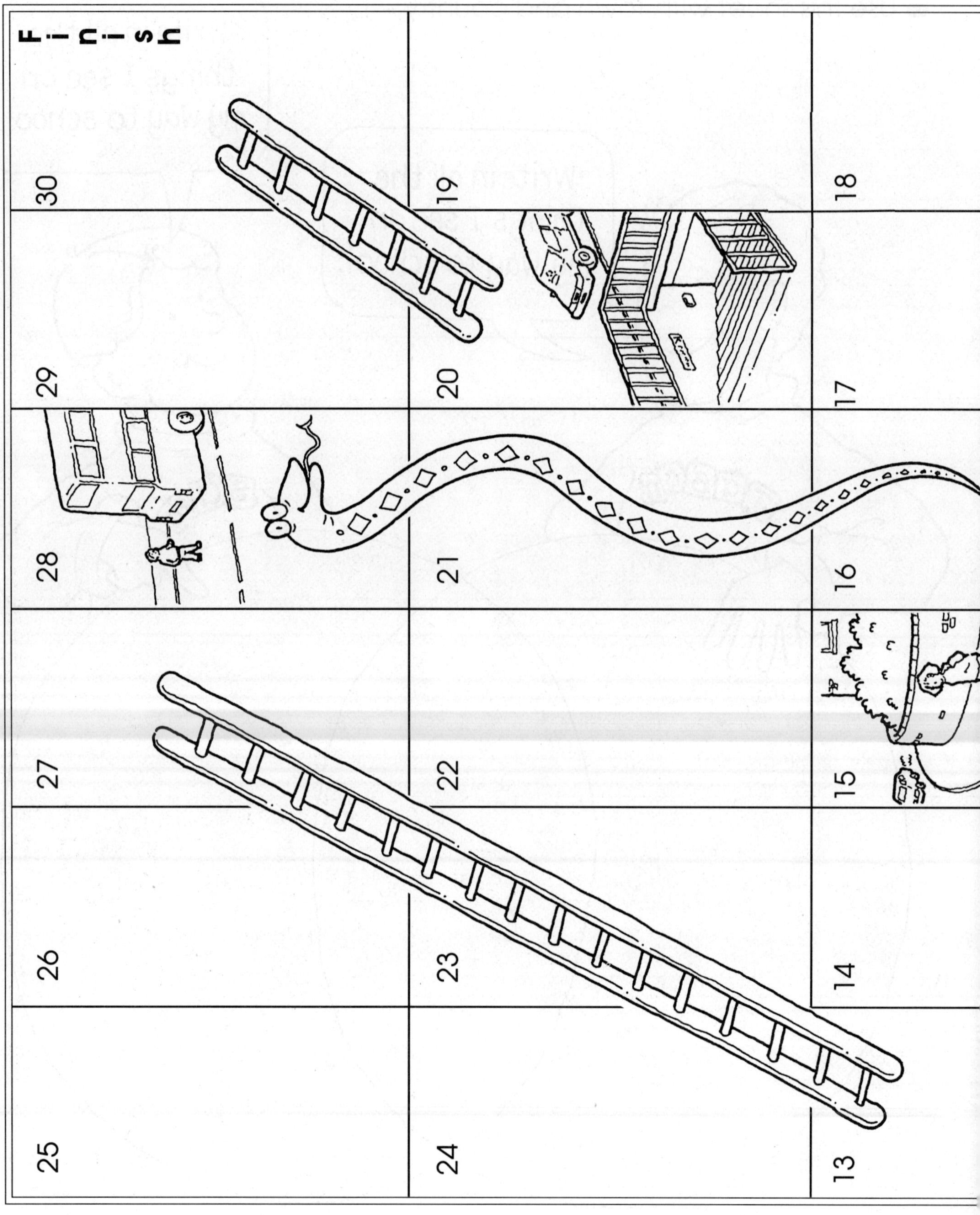

Name ______________________

Safety on journeys – 2

Name ____________________

People and journeys

- Colour in the pictures.
- Now cut them out and put them into pairs.

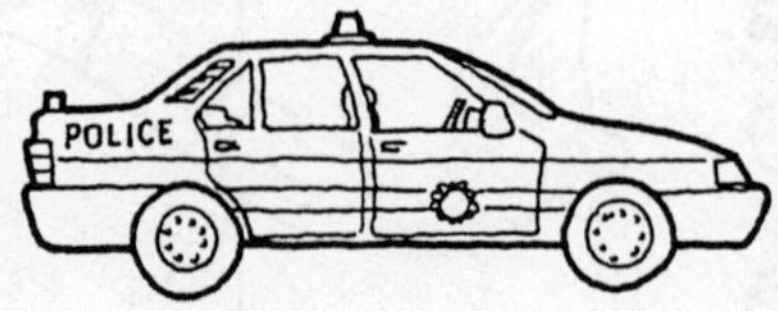

Letter to Switzerland

Ruth lives in London. She is sending a birthday present to her aunt in Switzerland.

- Colour in the pictures.
- Now cut them out and arrange them in order.

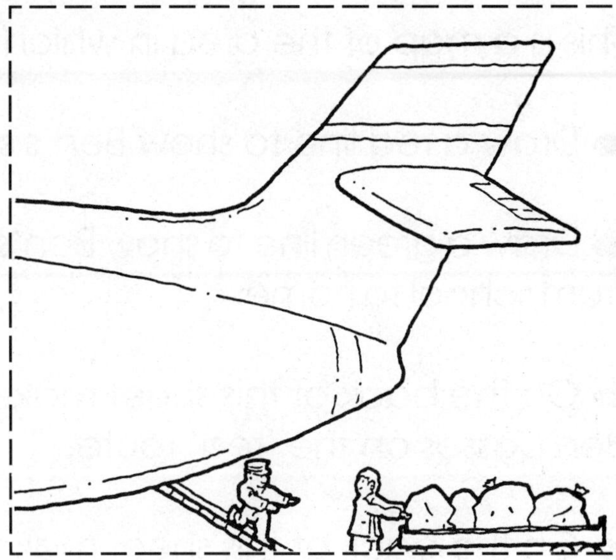

● Name ___________________________

Routes from Ben's home

This is a map of the area in which Ben lives.

● Draw a red line to show Ben's shortest route to school.

● Draw a green line to show Ben's longest route from school to home.

● On the back of this sheet make a list of all the things Ben passes on the 'red' route.

● On the back of this sheet make another list of things Ben passes on the 'green' route.

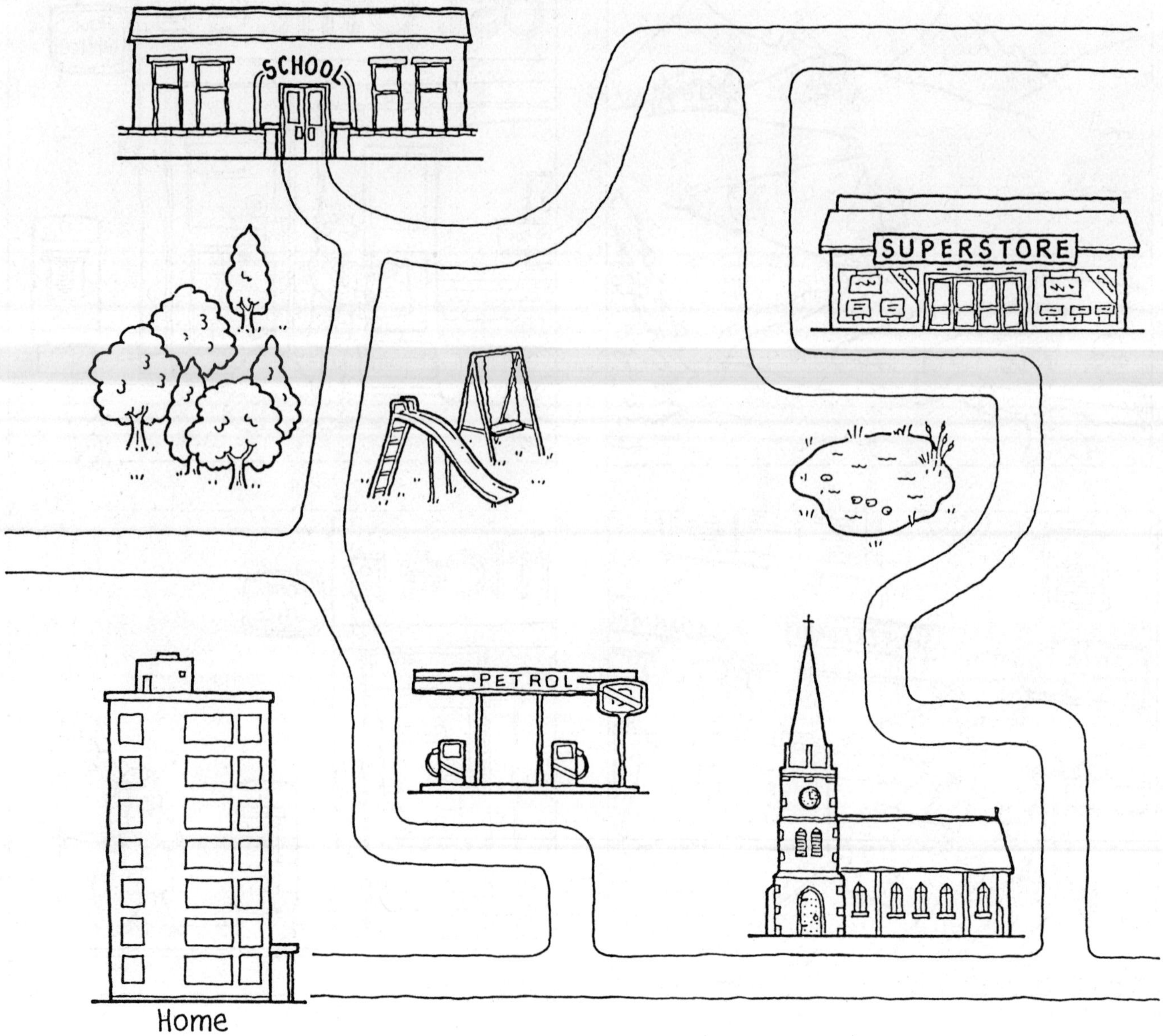

● Name ______________________________

Tracks and routes

● Look at the key and draw in the tracks of the bird, the frog and Mr Riley.

● Now complete the sentences below.

Mr Riley went to ______________________________

Lucy went to ______________________________

The bird went to ______________________________

The frog went to ______________________________

● Name ______________________

Journeys – 1

This is John's journey to the Post Office:

home
↓
garage
↓
shop
↓
woods
↓
post office

Name ______________________

Journeys – 2

- Use this sheet to record your journeys.

From ______ To ______ ______ ______ ______ ______ ______	From ______ To ______ ______ ______ ______ ______ ______
From ______ To ______ ______ ______ ______ ______ ______	From ______ To ______ ______ ______ ______ ______ ______

● Name ______________________

The crash

● Look at the pictures below. Can you draw pictures in the empty boxes to complete the story?

● Now can you write the story in words?

Houses and homes

Contents

Teachers' notes	1	Different homes	19
Parts of a house	5	Christmas parcels – 1	20
The front door	6	Christmas parcels – 2	21
Animal homes	7	Different rooms – 1	22
The letter	8	Different rooms – 2	23
Lucy's day	9	Pets	24
Pet jigsaws	10	On the fence	25
Machine jigsaws	11	Catching the burglar	26
In the garden	12	Cat on the roof	27
Family breakfast	13	House and garden – 1	28
Ben's house	14	House and garden – 2	29
Where we live	15	Family size – 1	30
Riddles – 1	16	Family size – 2	31
Riddles – 2	17	The storm	32
In the home	18		

Teachers' notes

The activities in this book aim to support the implementation of the National Curriculum for geography, Attainment Targets 2 and 4, Levels 1 to 3. These activities are not designed as teaching tools in their own right, but rather they offer the opportunity to practise newly-acquired knowledge and skills. It is important to explain the purpose of each activity at the start so that children can focus on that aspect of the task.

Aims of this book

- To highlight the many different types of houses and homes.
- To develop children's knowledge and vocabulary in relation to houses and homes.
- To introduce children to key ideas and knowledge about houses and homes.
- To provide opportunities to practise basic skills in English and mathematics within the context of a study of houses and homes.
- To encourage children to think about the address of their home and why it is important that each home has one.
- To look at the types of activities which take place at home.

Reproducing the activities

Most activities can be photocopied on to white paper, but in some cases (such as 8, 10, 11, 20 and 21) copying on to coloured paper may well be beneficial. Similarly copying on to card for pages 10, 11, 20 and 21 can provide a valuable resource, especially if the sheets are covered in clear, sticky plastic.

Geographical background

The study of houses and homes is a fundamental part of the local geography of every child. Houses and homes are the basis from which the children venture out to explore the environment. In the early years, places such as school, the park or the shops are located in relation to the home, that is how far or near they are, in terms of both time and distance. The home helps children to make sense of the rest of their environment and gives them a sense of perspective.

Activities which focus on homes, particularly the children's own homes will need sensitive handling. It is important to stress that not all children have two parents and live in a four-bedroom detached house! Each type of home (caravan, flat, maisonette, terraced house, semi-detached, etc) has its own merits and the activities in this book are designed to preclude any value judgements on the relative merits of the different types. Rather, the emphasis is on everyday activities or information which will be common to all homes, irrespective of the type of building.

The activities also include ideas about animal homes and this extends to pets (pages 7, 10 and 19). The aim is to encourage children to think about other creatures' need for homes, as well as dealing with the sharing of our homes with our pets. Similarly, key ideas on how activities in the home change throughout the day (page 9) are an important part of developing children's knowledge about houses and homes.

Other important points are developing ideas about the different rooms in homes, their different purposes and how this requires different furniture (pages 22 and 23).

At this stage it is important for children to develop knowledge and ideas about their own homes and those of their classmates. Studies of homes in other countries (see *Hot Places* in this series) and other environments should come later once the groundwork has been established.

Notes on individual activities

Page 5: Parts of a house

Aim: to familiarise the children with the names of key parts of the house.
Preparation and practice: before they start the activity, encourage the children to describe the picture and to name the different parts of the house.
Extension: draw a picture of another type of home, such as a flat and name its different parts.

Page 6: The front door

Aim: to encourage children to look more carefully and critically at aspects of their home, starting with the front door.
Preparation and practice: be sure children can identify the main features of the door shown, including the letter box, number and door knob. Talk to them about the front door of their own home and what features they will need to include on their picture.
Extension: ask the children to name their favourite/least favourite feature of their front door. Draw the front door of a friend.

Page 7: Animal homes

Aim: to encourage children to think about the different types of homes that animals use.
Preparation and practice: discuss class pets such as gerbils or goldfish and the homes in which they live, as well as the animals and homes shown in the pictures and animals in the wild.
Extension: on the pictures of animal homes mark features which keep out the rain and keep in the heat.

Page 8: The letter

Aim: to ensure that children know their own address and understand what the parts of the address mean.
Preparation and practice: show the children a large version of a letter addressed to the school, highlighting the different parts of the address – name, number, street, town and county. Discuss the reason for including all this information in an address, then look at their own addresses. In some cases it may be best to work backwards from the county to the street.
Extension: address letters to friends or relatives.

Page 9: Lucy's day

Aim: to highlight regular movements to and from the home and how these vary with time.
Preparation and practice: discuss with the children what they do at different times of the day – from getting up in the morning to going to bed at night. They can sequence the pictures in a straight line, or in a circle like a clock face, linked to specific times.
Extension: draw a picture to show a school day and a day at the weekend. How are they different?

Pages 10 and 11: Pet jigsaws/ Machine jigsaws

Aim: to encourage children to think about the contents of homes – the things that are found inside besides themselves and their parents.
Preparation and practice: the pictures at the top of the page should help children to match the jigsaw pieces.
Extension: make jigsaws of furniture at home for friends to complete.

Pages 12 and 13: In the garden/ Family breakfast

Aim: to highlight the range of activities that take place in homes, and encourage children to imagine events and conversations which might take place.
Preparation and practice: discuss what is happening in each scene and what the people might be saying before starting the activity.
Extension: suggest what else the people might be saying. Draw other scenes in the home, such as people watching TV or playing computer games, and write speech bubbles to show what they are saying.

Page 14: Ben's house

Aim: to link the three-dimensional and two-dimensional images of house shapes and enable children to see these links more clearly.
Preparation and practice: colour in the roof, front door and windows then cut out the shape and make the house.
Extension: use the houses to make a street, or village, on a layout which shows features such as a stream, or a hill. Can the children draw other shapes to cut out and assemble?

Page 15: Where we live

Aim: to encourage children to consider the wide range of different types of houses and homes.

Preparation and practice: discuss what the pictures show (i.e. different types of house) and point out the main differences, such as flats being in a block, and semi-detached being joined together. This is necessary to ensure that children can correctly identify their own home.
Extension: ask the children to draw the houses that are in their street. Do they know someone who lives in the type of house that has not been matched?

Pages 16 and 17: Riddles – 1 and 2

Aim: to encourage children to consider the different types of equipment found in the home and their various uses.
Preparation and practice: discuss the characteristics of various household objects and go on to write short descriptive texts based on everyday items found in the home.
Extension: write riddles for friends using objects found in the home.

Pages 18 and 19: In the home/ Different homes

Aim: to highlight the different functions and equipment of different parts of the home.
Preparation and practice: discuss what is shown in each picture before starting these activities. Explain to the children that they need to cut out the sentences and stick them under the appropriate picture.
Extension: draw other pictures of rooms and of homes and write sentences to go with them.

Pages 20 and 21: Christmas parcels – 1 and 2

Aim: to enable children to think about sorting parcels in the context of a small group.
Preparation and practice: it may be helpful to let the children practise sorting using dummy parcels labelled with the names of children in the class. Once they understand what is involved they can cut out the parcels and deliver them to the correct person.
Extension: write letters to the people in the picture and sort the letters.

Pages 22 and 23: Different rooms – 1 and 2

Aim: to highlight the different types of furniture to be found in different rooms.
Preparation and practice: the objects from Different rooms – 1 need to be cut out and matched with the diagram on Different rooms – 2. The teacher may want to point out that some objects, like the portable radio, could be found in both rooms, and discuss with children those objects that are specific to particular rooms.
Extension: draw pictures of other objects found in the home and stick them on to the diagram.

Page 24: Pets

Aim: to develop children's sorting abilities.
Preparation and practice: encourage the children to choose their own categories when sorting out the pets, for example two legs or four legs, stripes, dots, and so on.
Extension: draw other animals which are found at home, for example gerbils, budgies, goldfish, and sort them.

Page 25: On the fence

Aim: to encourage children to look at the many different types of boundaries to be found around homes and properties.
Preparation and practice: talk to the children about the type of fences found around their home. In particular, discuss what such fences are made of, such as hedges, wood, bricks or concrete.
Extension: discuss why fences are useful and why they can also be a nuisance.

Page 26: Catching the burglar

Aim: to look at dramatic activities which may take place around the home.
Preparation and practice: before the children start to write the story discuss with them what is happening in each picture. Give some thought to a title for the story and how this might affect the ending.
Extension: invent other dramatic activities that may take place around the home.

Page 27: Cat on the roof

Aim: to develop awareness of some of the dangers around the home.
Preparation and practice: point out to the children the need to relate the pictures they draw to the text. Similarly, stress the importance of writing concisely what the printed picture shows in clear, short sentences. Discuss how the story might develop and which details can be represented in the drawings and which by text.
Extension: write sentences and draw pictures of other events around the home, for example the chip pan catches fire!

Pages 28 and 29: House and garden – 1 and 2

Aim: to develop awareness of scale in relation to sorting elements inside the home and in the garden.
Preparation and practice: discuss what is shown in each picture and how they will need to be arranged to fit on the Carroll diagram.
Extension: draw other different-sized objects from house and garden and stick them on the Carroll diagram.

Pages 30 and 31: Family size – 1 and 2

Aim: to highlight the way in which the scale of items in the home is related to the people who live there.
Preparation and practice: point out that babies do not eat with a knife and fork, but use a small spoon, how they sit in a high chair and sleep in a cot. Discuss similarities and differences between adults and children of four or five in terms of furniture and cutlery. On the Carroll diagram one item fits into each space.
Extension: draw other items for the people on the chart and stick them on the Carroll diagram.

Page 32: The storm

Aim: to encourage children to think about how houses protect them from the weather, and how extremes of weather can damage the houses.
Preparation and practice: discuss with the children the ways in which houses provide protection from the weather – the walls, roof, windows and door. Look at the effects of very severe weather and how families might cope with the resulting problems.
Extension: draw the effects of a flood on a house built on a river bank.

National Curriculum: Geography

The activities in this book support the following requirements of the PoS for KS1 from the geography National Curriculum:

Geographical skills
Pupils should be taught to:
- make representations of actual or imaginary places;
- use pictures and photographs to identify features.

Places and themes
Pupils should be taught to:
- identify and name familiar features in the local area;
- investigate the use of land and buildings in the local area;
- talk about work and leisure activities.

Physical geography
Pupils should be taught to:
- investigate the effects of weather on themselves and their surroundings.

Human geography
Pupils should be taught:
- the uses made of buildings in the local area and further afield;
- an awareness of how goods and services needed by the community are provided.

Environmental geography
Pupils should be taught:
- where common materials are obtained;
- to discuss and explain their likes and dislikes about features of their environment.

Scottish Curriculum 5 – 14 Environmental Studies: Social Subjects

Attainment outcome	Strand	Target	Level
Understanding people and places	Knowledge and understanding	Aspects of the physical and built environment. Ways in which places have affected people and people have used and affected places.	A
	Recording and presenting	Record collected evidence by drawing pictures, making models and writing captions and short pieces.	A

Name ______________________

Parts of a house

- Can you match the words with the objects in the picture?

chimney **roof** **door**

wall **window** **drainpipe**

- Colour in the house.

Name ______________________

The front door

- This is Mary's front door.
- Colour the letter box red.
- Colour the door knob black.
- Colour each of the panels.
- Now draw your own front door in the space below.

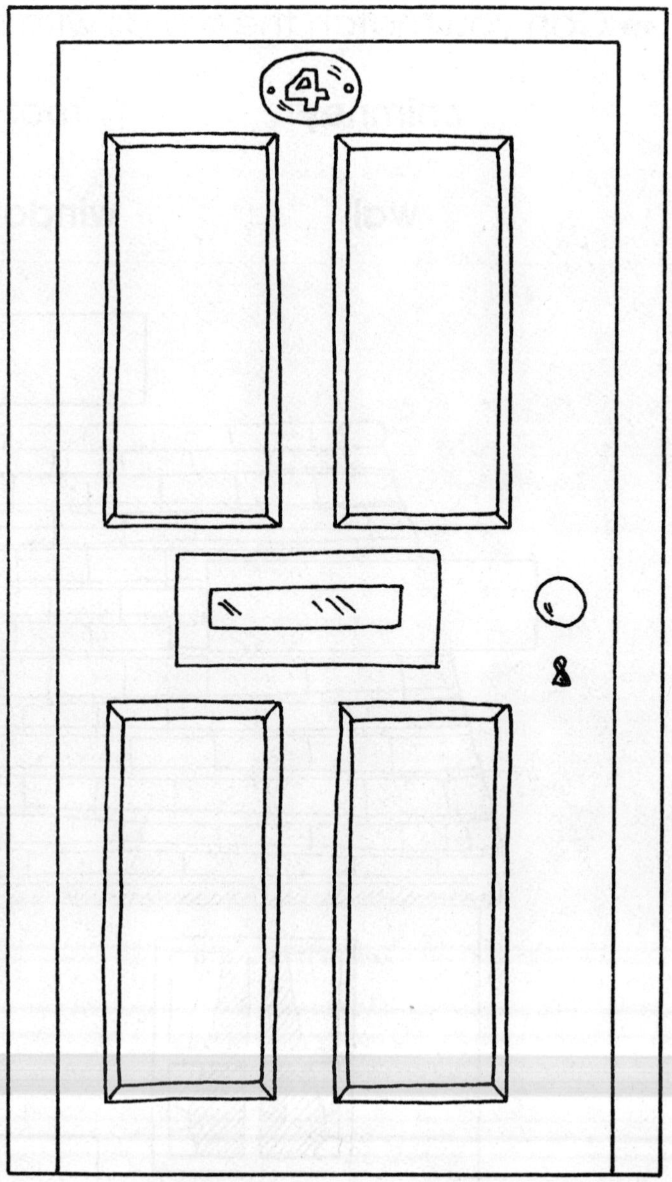

Name ______________________

Animal homes

- Draw a line linking each animal or bird with its home.

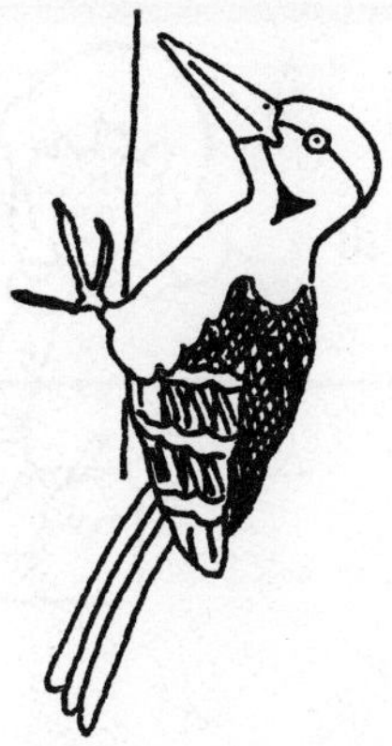

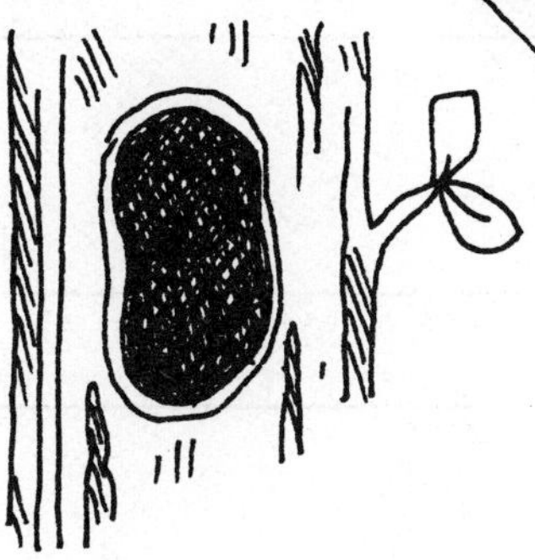

- Now draw another animal in the box on the left and draw its home next to it. Can you think of others to draw?

Name ______________________

The letter

- Fill in the address on the letter.
- In box A write your name.
- In boxes B and C write the number of your house and the name of the road.
- In box D write the name of the town.
- In box E write the name of the county.

A

B

C

D

E

Name ______________________________

Lucy's day

The pictures show how Lucy spends her day.

- Colour them in then cut them out and put them in order.

Name ____________________

Pet jigsaws

- Two pet jigsaws have been muddled together. Cut out the pieces and complete the jigsaws.

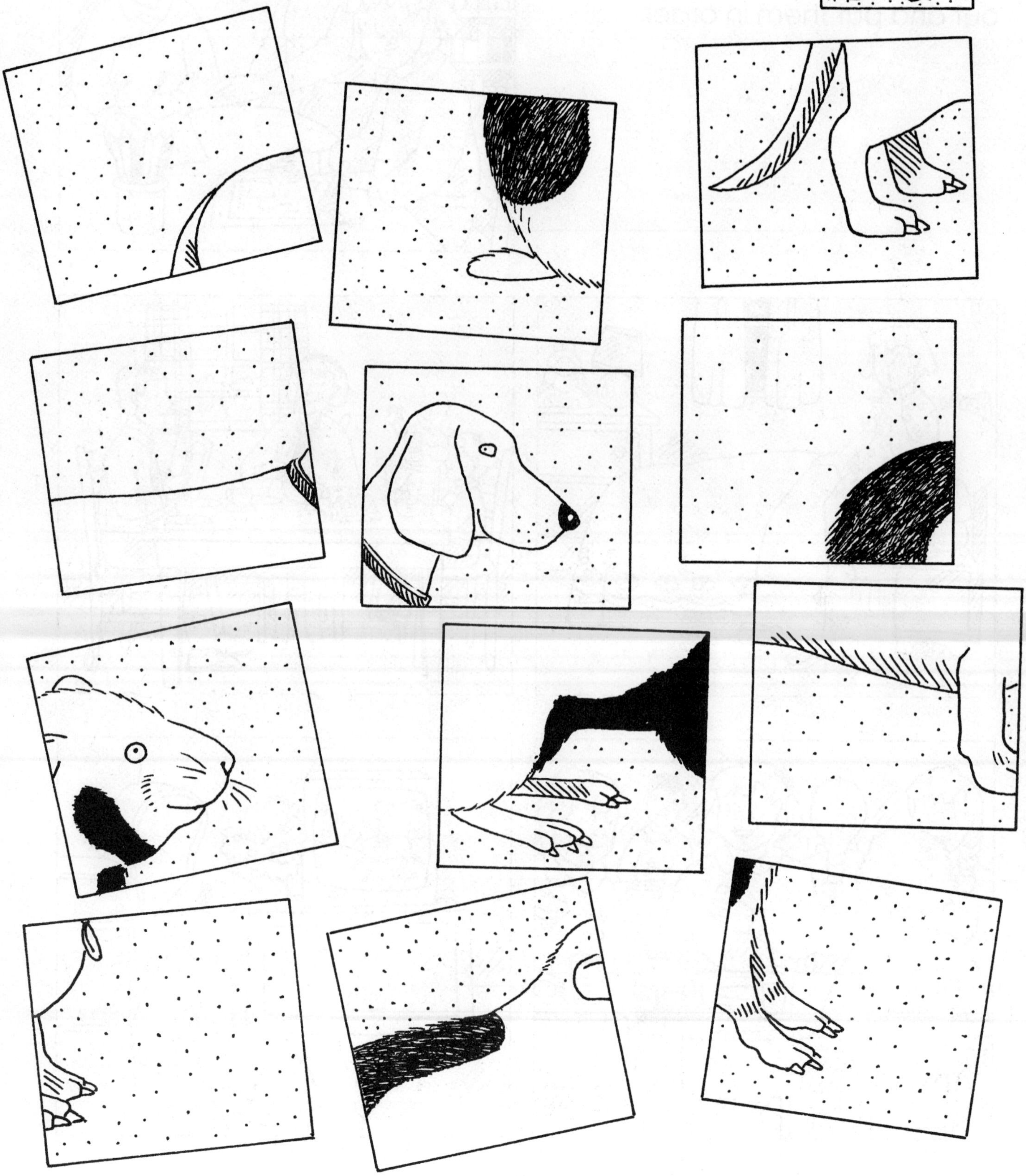

Name ______________________

Machine jigsaws

- Two machine jigsaws have been muddled together. Cut out the pieces and complete the jigsaws.

Name ______________________

In the garden

- Look at the picture. What are the people saying? Write their words in the speech bubbles.

Name ______________________

Family breakfast

- Look at the picture. What are the people saying? Write their words in the speech bubbles.

Name ______________________

Ben's house

- Colour in the house below.
- Now cut it out and cut slits to make tabs.
- Fold along the dotted lines.
- Now can you make the house as shown in the picture on the right?

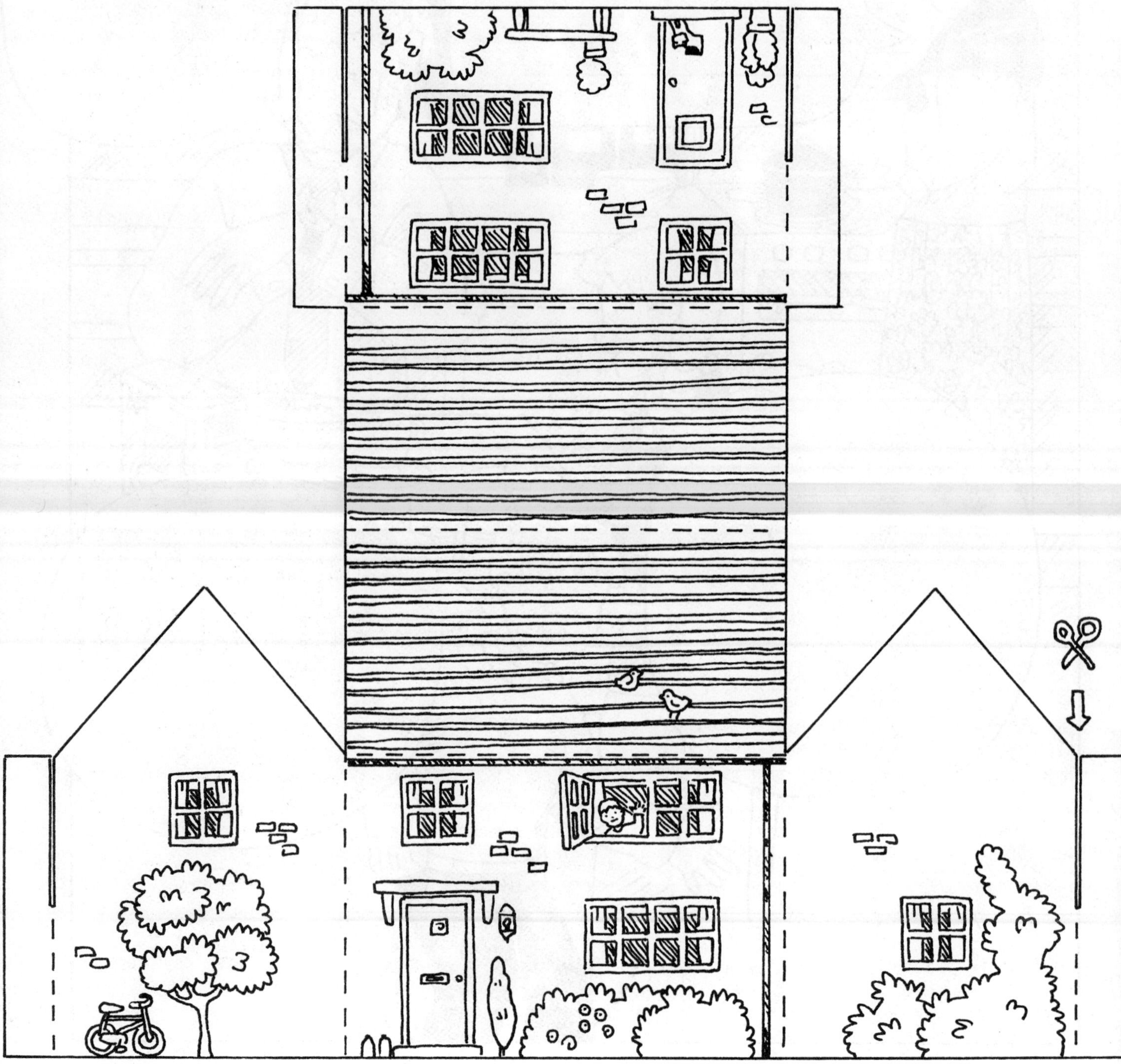

Name ____________________

Where we live

- Draw a picture of yourself in the first box.
- Now draw a friend in each of the other boxes.
- Match the people with the type of home in which they live.

detached

semi-detached

terraced

flats

Name ______________________

Riddles – 1

- Read the riddles and write in the answers.

I suck up dirt. I use electricity. You can push me. I am a ______________	I have four wheels. You can drive me. People go to school in me. I am a ______________

- Can you write in the riddles for the objects below?

____

____

____

I am a washing machine

____

____

____

I am a telephone

____

____

____

I am a television

____

____

____

I am a bed

Name ______________________________

Riddles – 2

- Read the riddles and write in the answers.

I boil water. I switch myself off. I plug into the electricity. I am a ______________	I keep people warm. They wear me on their head. I am made of cloth. I am a ______________

- Can you write in the riddles for the objects below?

____

____

____

I am a toaster

____

____

____

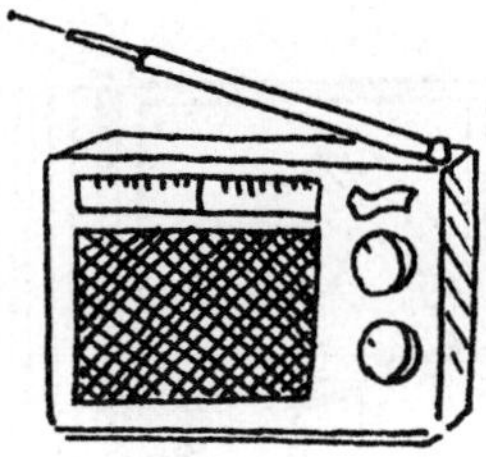

I am a radio

____

____

____

I am a computer

____

____

____

I am an iron

Name ______________________________

In the home

- Look at the pictures and sentences below.
- Now cut out the sentences and match them to the pictures.

I am in the bedroom.
I am wearing pyjamas.

I am in the garage.
The car is not going well
so I am repairing it.

I am in the kitchen.
I am thirsty so I am having
a drink.

I am in the study. I am
working on my computer.

Name ________________________

Different homes

- Look at the pictures and sentences below.

- Now cut out the sentences and match them to the pictures.

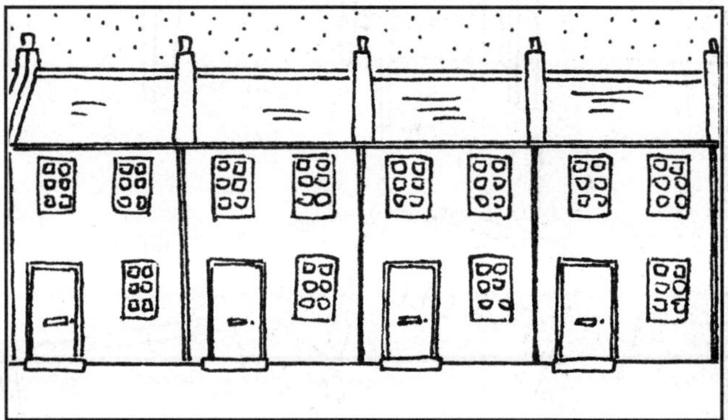

I live in a cottage.
It has a thatched roof.

I live in a flat.
It is on the third floor
of our block.

I live in a terraced house.
It is joined to lots of
other houses.

I live in a cage.
It has bars and a wheel.

Name ______________________

Christmas parcels – 1

- Use this sheet with Christmas parcels – 2.

- These are Christmas presents for Class One.
Cut them out and sort the parcels.

Name ______________________

Christmas parcels – 2

Use this sheet with Christmas parcels – 1.

- Help the children collect their parcels.

Stick them in the correct sacks.

Name ______________________________

Different rooms – 1

- Colour in the objects below.

- Now cut them out and stick them into the room where they belong on Different rooms – 2.

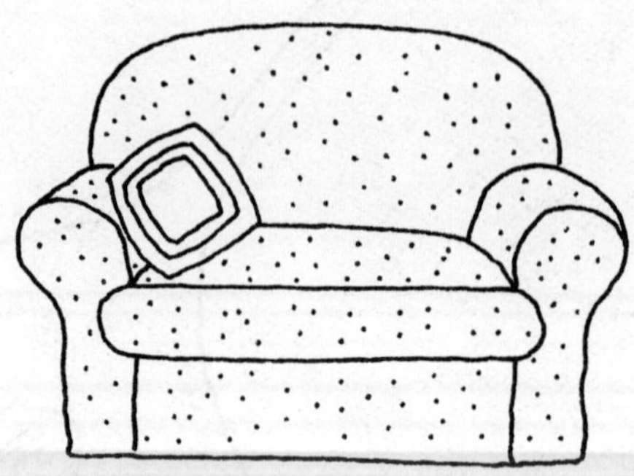

Name ______________________

Different rooms – 2

- Use this sheet with Different rooms – 1.

Name ______________________

Pets

- Cut out the pets and sort them into groups.

Name ______________________

On the fence

- Look at the pictures and words below.
Can you match the words with the correct picture?

tall wooden fence **brick wall** **chain link fence**

hedge **railings** **low wooden fence**

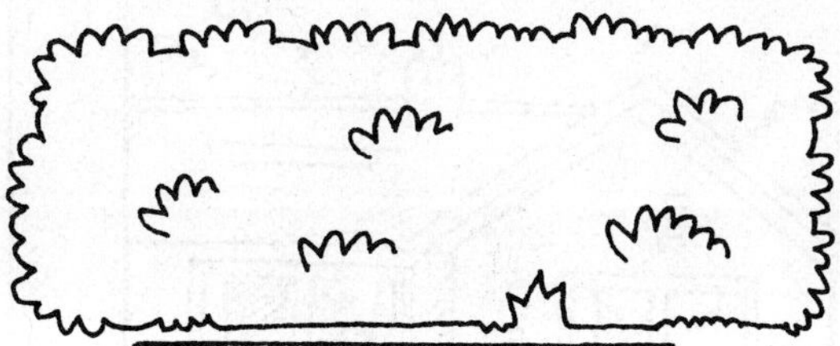

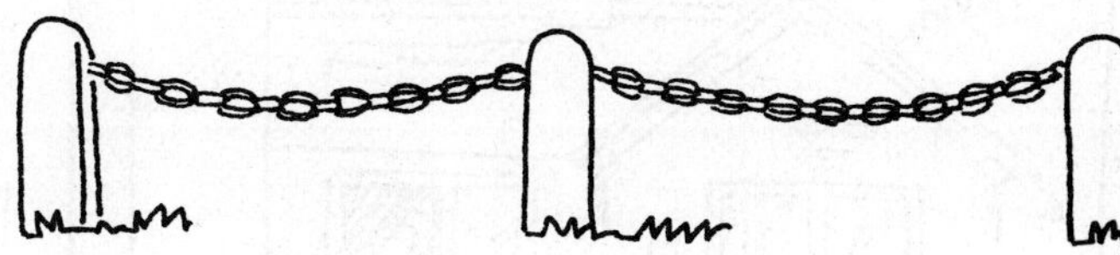

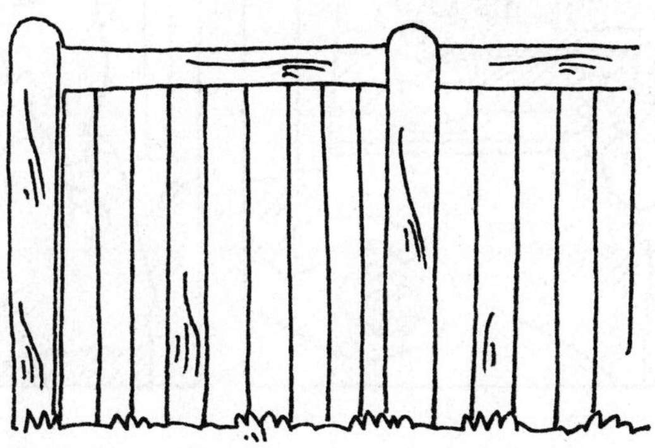

- Colour in each type of fence.

- Now draw some other types of fence.

Name ____________________

Catching the burglar

- Look at the pictures below. Draw a picture in the empty box to complete the story.

- Now write the story shown in the pictures and give it a title.

Name ______________________

Cat on the roof

- Draw in the missing pictures and write the missing text. Now finish the story off in the last box.

One day the cat climbed the tree. Then she jumped on to the roof of the house.	____________________ ____________________ ____________________ ____________________

Suddenly the ladder fell away and dad was stuck on the roof. Then the fire engine arrived.	____________________ ____________________ ____________________ ____________________

● Name ______________________________

House and garden – 1

- Colour in the objects below.

- Match the labels with the objects. Now look at the Carroll diagram on House and garden – 2.

wardrobe **settee** **trowel**

tree **telephone** **radio** **bucket**

lawn mower **cup and saucer**

Name ________________________

House and garden – 2

Use this sheet with House and garden – 1.

- Sort the objects into the correct groups and write their names in the diagram below.

	in the house	in the garden
large		
small		

Name ______________________

Family size – 1

- Look at the pictures below.

- Can you match the labels with the objects?

Now look at the Carroll diagram on Family size – 2.

baby's spoon	**cot**	**small chair**
large chair	**large bed**	**baby's high chair**
small bed	**small knife and fork**	**large knife and fork**

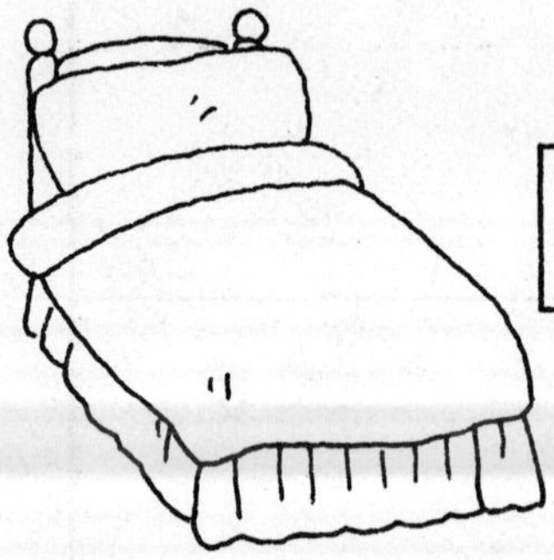

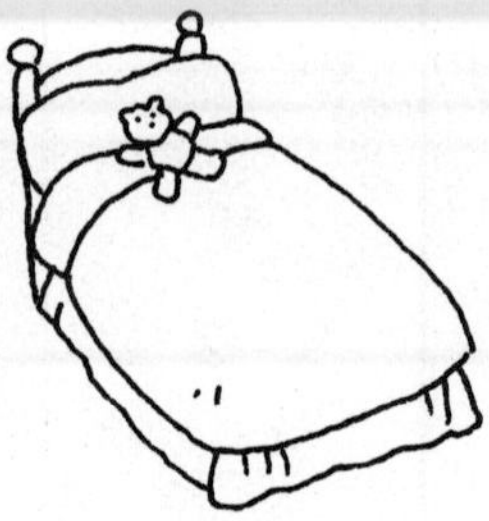

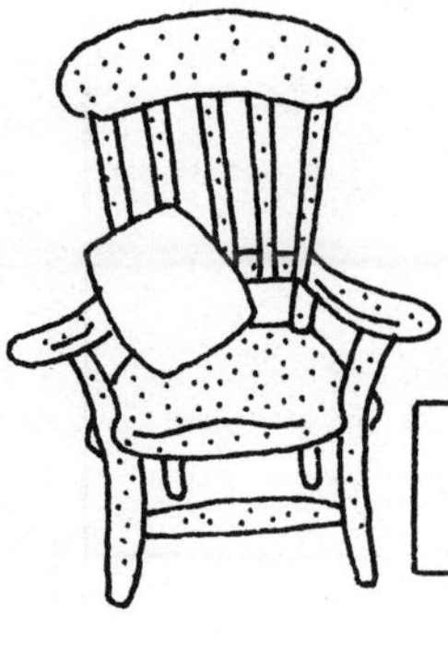

● Name ___________________________

Family size – 2

Use this sheet with Family size – 1.

● Sort the objects into the correct groups and write their names in the diagram below.

	bed	things to eat with	chair
mum			
child aged 4-5			
baby			

Name ______________________________

The storm

- Look at the pictures below. Draw a picture in the empty box to complete the story.

- Write out the story shown in the pictures and give your story a title.